NATIONAL PARKS OF
AMERICA

Donald Young

LONGMEADOW
PRESS

This book was designed and produced by
by Todtri Productions Limited
P.O. Box 20058
New York, NY 10023-1482

Printed and Bound in Singapore

Library of Congress Catalog Card Number 94-075238

ISBN 0-681-45399-0

Author: Donald Young

Producer: Robert M. Tod
Book Designer: Mark Weinberg
Production Coordinator: Heather Weigel
Photo Editor: Edward Douglas
Editor: Mary Forsell, Joanna Wissinger, Don Kennison
Design Associate: Jackie Skroczky

CONTENTS

INTRODUCTION

February. The snow is deep and the air bitterly cold. It numbs your fingertips and crinkles the hairs in your nostrils. In front of you, steam and hot bubbly water rise from the ground. You are close enough to feel the warmth but far enough away to avoid being scalded.

The steam forms a white curtain before your eyes, but you soon realize that you are not alone. Deeper sounds, snorts and grunts, intrude on the hissing and cheerful whistling of the small geyser. Dark forms move beyond the curtain of steam. Large black hairy beasts, their visible breath mingling with the steam, struggle through the snow. They have come to this spot to seek relief from the cold and to nibble on plants nourished by the heat of the geyser.

These are American bison, also called buffalo, and this is Yellowstone National Park in winter.

A store that sold camping equipment once had as its slogan, "Before you go, you dream." Next to the slogan was a drawing of a hiker wearing a pack and looking off into the distance. Dreams of wilderness adventure can still come true in the United States, and in fact these dreams had their beginning at Yellowstone, the first national park in the United States—and in the world.

Until the seventeenth century, the future United States was, of course, one vast park. By then, Europe had been settled and the populations of Asia were filling up that continent. But the Western Hemisphere, though "discovered" by Columbus in 1492, remained largely unmarked by its relatively small number of native inhabitants.

From the time Europeans began settling on the East Coast in the early 1600s, the transformation of their adopted country occurred quickly. Whether fleeing political or religious persecution, or else lured by the prospect of better economic opportunities across the sea, they had chosen to make their home in the New World. And, as Professor Roderick Nash has written, "Wilderness, after all, was what had made the New World new."

But if wilderness offered the untrammeled freedom pioneers had never known in Europe, it also presented many dangers, including hostile Indians and wild animals. The wilds were also perceived as a barrier to "progress," by which was usually meant the opportunity to earn a living.

Hence, across the land, from the forests of New England to the mountains and valleys of Appalachia, to the Midwest and to the edges of the Great Plains, the snap of an axe followed by the crash of a tree carried from ridge to valley and signaled the arrival of civilization to once-virgin country. In the two-and-a-half centuries prior to 1872, when the first national park was proclaimed, most of the original American "park" had been chopped down and plowed over. Consequently, the creation of official parks were belated and imperfect attempts to preserve representative remnants of what once had been pristine wilderness.

Settlers suffered no sense of loss in the toppling of trees. After all, there was always more untouched timber beyond the next river, wasn't there? Besides, it was written in the Bible that mankind should increase in numbers, conquer the earth, and have dominion over other creatures. God was clearly on the side of Paul Bunyan and the plowman. Alexis de Tocqueville, during a visit to frontier Michigan in 1831, found Americans on "the march across these wilds, draining swamps, turning the course of rivers, peopling solitudes, and subduing nature." The 1890 Federal census confirmed that the frontier had disappeared, that the United States had been occupied from coast to coast, albeit thinly in many areas. But attitudes had already begun to change. In dirty, crowded, rapidly growing cities, citizens yearned to see something of what was left of the natural world, and actually wanted to experience the rugged outdoor life that their pioneer kinsmen had known. Many urban Americans had grown prosperous and had more free time than their country cousins. The concept of "vacation" had penetrated the American consciousness. From this class, the yuppies of their day, sprang the impetus for the creation of national parks.

Even before the 1890 census officially closed an era in American history, the preservation of parklands for posterity was well under way. Public gardens and city parks were an Old World feature adopted in the New. Then, in 1832, the artist George Catlin carried the concept of common ground a great step forward. Catlin,

a serious student of American Indian life, contributed greatly to our appreciation of the first Americans through his writing, paintings, and engravings. In the spring of 1832 he had traveled to present-day South Dakota to paint scenes of the Sioux nation. But he was dismayed by what he saw. The Sioux had proved unable to cope with the arrival of white men. Many of them drank heavily, and killed buffalo in order to trade the hides for whiskey.

Catlin was convinced that something had to be done, quickly. After he spent some time looking out over the prairie, he wrote that much of the West was "worthy of our preservation and protection." He called for the creation of "a magnificent park ... a Nation's Park, containing man and beast, in all the wild[ness] and freshness of their nature's beauty!"

In that same year, 1832, Congress approved the creation of the Hot Springs Reservation in Arkansas. At that site, forty-seven hot springs spilled forth water from deep underground. People with various ailments were coming from long distances to bathe in the hot water in the hope that the experience might improve their health. In creating the reservation, the United States also established the principle that a natural feature was worth protecting. Almost a century later, Hot Springs was redesignated as a national park.

The occasional visionary such as Catlin was gradually joined by other Americans who questioned the unthinking despoliation of so much of the land. For one thing, some religious leaders had second thoughts about the Biblical sanction for taming the wild. They questioned whether God, the Creator of the universe and of all the plants and animals, wanted humans to overrun nature and bend it to their own convenience. They also argued that God showed His love for us through creation of the natural world.

The writer Henry David Thoreau thought we were losing something very important to us as we continued to chop down the forests. In 1851 he put it in eight beautiful words: "In wildness is the preservation of the world." He was convinced that opportunities to enjoy wild nature would make all of us more alive, stronger in body and spirit.

Scientists spoke up, too. With the passing years, more young people were being trained as biologists and botanists, and they urged that nature be preserved for scientific study. They realized that many species of plants and animals were becoming rare or even disappearing altogether.

Some thoughtful Americans began to ask themselves "What makes us different, special?" The U.S. tradition of political and religious freedom was the most obvious answer. But Americans were also a little defensive. Europe's many cathedrals, museums, and classical antiquities embodied a centuries-long cultural heritage. In contrast, America's cultural development was still in its infancy.

However, Americans had something Europeans did not have: a vast, sparsely populated country, with jagged mountain peaks, tumbling rivers, seemingly bottomless canyon gorges, and bountiful wildlife. Europe was fully populated, with only a few areas remaining in their natural state. Could not America's natural wonders become its cathedrals, its monuments? In a land where no man may rule as king, the great western parks would some day commonly be called the crown jewels of the United States.

In 1864, Congress gave Yosemite Valley to California and instructed the state to create a state park. In this way, formal protection was first given to the enchanting corridor through the High Sierras 150 miles east of San Francisco. Just a few years later, the world's first national park became a reality.

For decades, grizzled prospectors and "mountain men" had explored the land near the headwaters of the Yellowstone River. When they went back East and told of smoking fumaroles, geysers spewing hot water hundreds of feet in the air, and swirling pools of minerals in a rainbow of colors, people said they were delirious. But these and many other "rumors" from the West proved to be true.

The federal government sent an expedition into the region in 1870, with civilians being escorted by the U.S. Cavalry. They gazed upon Yellowstone Falls, Yellowstone Lake, and the geyser basins. As the men on horseback emerged from a dense lodgepole pine forest and entered an open valley, a geyser "performed" for them as they approached it. They named it "Old Faithful." Today, this geyser remains the symbol of the park.

On the historic night of September 19, 1870, near the confluence of the Gibbon and Firehole rivers, the men sat around a campfire, discussing what they had seen. Several said that they intended to stake claims around the geysers so they could charge tourists who would pay to see them. But another man, Cornelius Hedges, later a judge in the Montana Territory, objected, arguing that Yellowstone "ought to be set apart as a great National Park." One of his companions at the campfire, Nathaniel P. Langford, lay awake that night thinking over the idea. Embracing the cause, he spent the next few months publicizing Yellowstone and urging Congress to approve a park. In doing so, he challenged the nearly universal assumption of the time that all of the public domain should be sold or given away.

Ferdinand Hayden, director of the Geological and Geographical Survey of the Territories, led a second expedition into the area in 1871. The painter Thomas Moran and the photographer William Henry Jackson went with him. Perhaps more than anything else, Jackson's photographs convinced Congress and the public that a park must be established. In 1872 Congress passed and President Ulysses S. Grant signed into law a bill that created Yellowstone National Park. The law described Yellowstone as "a public park or pleasuring ground for the benefit and enjoyment of the people."

Many congressmen and newspaper writers had little understanding of the geological features that were being protected. They were often referred to as "curiosities," "decorations," and "freaks."

The automobile had not yet been invented, but the Northern Pacific Railroad had big plans for transporting tourists to the park, and it therefore became an enthusiastic supporter of Yellowstone. The Northern Pacific and other railroads sometimes pressed for commercial development inside the parks that was not always suitable for them. But the railroads deserve much of the credit for introducing the early parks to the American people.

In Yellowstone's early years, visitors had true wilderness experiences. In 1877, the Seventh Cavalry pursued the great leader Chief Joseph and his band of Nez Perce through the park. The Indians grabbed two groups of campers, including a number of women, and took them along. The Nez Perce later allowed their white captives to escape through a landscape of spouting geysers and bubbling mudpots.

Despite having been "protected," Yellowstone at first was anybody's park. Sportsmen shot bison and ranchers let their cattle graze within the park boundaries. Visitors teased the geysers, some even shaking soap flakes into the vents in hopes of provoking an eruption. In 1886, the Army was formally assigned responsibility for the park and the soldiers chased out the poachers and squatters. Unfortunately, the military, which was also put in charge of other early parks, demonstrated little understanding of the forces of nature. Believing that tourists wanted to see the large herbivores such as elk and deer, the soldiers killed the wolves, coyotes, and mountain lions that preyed on them. In turn, the browsing and grazing animals, no longer menaced by predators, multiplied in number. They outgrew their food supply and perished en masse from starvation. This tragic outcome was one of many painful lessons taught to humans who sought to "manage" nature.

The example of Yellowstone inspired railroads and other commercial interests banking on a profitable tourist trade to call for more parks. Such pressure, coupled with a growing public appetite for preserving the country's natural splendor, created a favorable climate in Congress for national park proposals. Today, more than fifty areas have been officially designated as national parks, but the efforts to establish them almost always met with resistance.

In fact, a common pattern emerged, one in which a lone individual typically devoted years to promoting a particular landscape with which he had fallen in love. Getting approval for a park was almost always a struggle, and the conflicts featured a cast of characters that seldom varied except in name: articulate naturalists asserting that the nation would shame itself if it failed to create a park, corporations fulminating against "locking up" resource-rich land, lumbermen and miners lamenting the possible loss of jobs, logrolling congressmen agreeing to support a park bill in return for some other favor, and an occasional generous millionaire buying up acreage and presenting it to the government for a park. Sometimes schoolchildren contributing nickels and dimes played a supporting role.

Yellowstone is in the Rocky Mountains, principally in Wyoming. The next chapters of the national parks story would be written in California, with John Muir, the prototypical lone crusader, a man willing, even eager, to devote his life to a single cause, as the hero of those chapters.

Muir was born in Scotland, but his family emigrated to the United States, and he spent the rest of his boyhood in Wisconsin. He was a Christian—a Calvinist—and his religious training said nothing about protecting nature. But Muir studied geology and botany at the University of Wisconsin, and he found order and harmony in the natural world. In the wilderness, unimproved by "civilization," everything had a purpose. Where less perceptive people could see only chaos and confusion, Muir saw a grand design created by God. In Muir's words, every species is "hitched to everything else in the universe."

In 1867, at age twenty-nine, while working in a factory in Indianapolis, Muir nearly lost his sight in an accident. Believing that God was telling him that it was time for him to enter the wilderness, Muir struck out on his own, hiking a thousand miles to the Gulf of Mexico. Then he headed west, to San Francisco. Telling a passerby that his next destination was "any place that is wild," Muir entered the wilderness of the Sierra Nevada, a mountain range in eastern California. ("Sierra" is a Spanish word describing a range with jagged peaks.)

When Muir first saw Yosemite Valley, it had already been made a state park. He immediately fell in love with the valley, and he would later write of "holy Yosemite." Millions of people now share Muir's belief that Yosemite Valley's seven miles offer the most lovely vista in the United States. During the Ice Age, thousands of years ago, mighty glaciers pushed through it and gouged out the broad U-shape. The high, hard, light-gray granite walls of the valley convey a feeling of power and strength. Yet when you gaze at them, you do not feel overwhelmed or menaced. They are perfectly proportioned, the magnum opus of a great sculptor.

In the spring, as the snow melts in the high country,

misty waterfalls spill icy water hundreds of feet onto the valley floor. Deer and other animals feed in the grassy valley and drink from the Merced River, whose current runs swiftly from the mountains. At the upper end of the valley, Mirror Lake is so smooth that it contains a perfect mirror image of the mountains rising above it.

Muir explored the vast, rugged mountain country above the valley. He was dismayed by the mess humans were making of the region. In the valley, inside the state park, hotels and other places of business had been built. Sheep—which he called "hoofed locusts"—and cattle ranged widely over the mountains, destroying and consuming wildflowers and other plants.

Muir, a skillful writer and promoter, resolved that the park at Yosemite must be expanded. Influential magazines published his articles. "Climb the mountains and get their good tidings," was his classic advice. "Nature's peace will flow into you as the sunshine into the trees. The winds will blow their freshness into you, and the storms their energy, while cares drop off like autumn leaves."

Muir's efforts, supported by others, finally paid off in 1890 when Congress approved a Yosemite National Park. The valley itself remained a state park until 1906, when the state returned it to federal control for inclusion in the national park.

To Muir's delight, Congress established two more national parks in the Sierra Nevada in 1890. Sequoia and General Grant parks protected stands of the giant sequoia trees. Lumber companies had their eyes on the trees, the world's heaviest living things. Both parks were later expanded to protect more of the trees and the rugged mountain country of the Sierra Nevada. The Grant park later became part of Kings Canyon National Park.

Owners of sheep and cattle were outraged when their animals were banished from Yosemite National Park. They sought to abolish it, or at least to reduce its boundaries. Robert Underwood Johnson, an editor of *Century Magazine* who had published Muir's articles, feared that the California parks might be in danger. He suggested to Muir that an organization of private citizens be formed to help defend them. Muir welcomed the idea of a club that could "do something for wildness and make the mountains glad." Some California university professors also wanted to form a club.

This new organization, the Sierra Club, was founded in 1892. The club's 182 charter members elected Muir president, a position he held for twenty-two years until his death. In the early years, most Sierrans lived in California, and they focused primarily on exploring and protecting the Sierra Nevada range. Nowadays, with more than 500,000 members nationwide, the organization seeks to make the American people aware of many different threats to the environment, such as acid rain and toxic waste. The Sierra Club has won many victories over the years, but its first was one of its most important. It helped defeat an attempt by stockmen to reduce the size of Yosemite by one-half.

Two mountains created by volcanic eruptions became national parks at the turn of the century. The first, Mount Rainier, an ice-covered peak that soars above dense forests and flowered subalpine meadows southeast of Seattle, joined the list in 1899.

Crater Lake came next, and its eventual elevation to national park status provides a case study illustrating how one person can make a difference. One day in 1870, as a Kansas schoolboy eating his lunch, William Gladstone Steel glanced at the newspaper in which his mother had wrapped the food. It contained an article that told an incredible story. About seven thousand years ago in far-off Oregon, near the Pacific Ocean, a massive volcanic explosion had collapsed the mountaintop and sent ash spewing some seven hundred miles to the east. The sky must have been black for days. The explosion had left a crater inside the mountain, and inside the crater a beautiful deep blue lake had formed.

Steel decided he had to see that lake. Many years later, as an adult, he stood at the rim at last, gazing across a bright blue expanse of water, six miles wide. At 1,932 feet in depth, Crater Lake is the deepest lake in the United States. Steel spent the next seventeen years of his life trying to make the mountain a national park. Using up much of his money, he lectured, lobbied, wrote articles, and circulated petitions. Congress finally responded to his appeals, and Crater Lake National Park was approved in 1902.

Of all the magnificent scenery still without protection as a park at the dawn of the twentieth century, the Grand Canyon of the Colorado River was undoubtedly the most striking. Spanish explorers had seen the canyon in 1540, but the mile-deep gorge had gradually worked its way into the public's consciousness only in the latter half of the nineteenth century.

In 1857, a U.S. surveying party led by Lt. Joseph Ives traveled up the Colorado River in a steamboat to search for the canyon. Ives finally saw what we now call the Grand Canyon. Although he thought it beautiful, Ives could not imagine anyone else would want to come there. In his report to the government, he wrote: "Ours has been the first, and will doubtless be the last, party of whites to visit this profitless locality." Seldom has a prediction been so wrong.

Major John Wesley Powell fought in the Union Army during the Civil War and lost an arm. Despite his handicap, his spirit of adventure was very much alive. In 1869, he led an expedition down the Colorado River and through the Grand Canyon. The trip by Powell and his men in their wooden boats was one of the last great journeys of exploration in the United States. It took the men two months just to travel from southern Wyoming, through Utah, to the eastern edge of the canyon in Arizona.

As they looked ahead and saw the walls of the abyss rising many thousands of feet, the men were worried. So far as they knew, no one had ever traveled through the canyon before. Their only food was bread, bacon, dried fruit, and coffee. The temperature was as high as 115°F. In an entry in his book, dated August 13, Powell wrote: "We are now ready to start on our way down the Great Unknown…. We are three-quarters of a mile in the depths of the earth, and the great river shrinks into insignificance, as it dashes its angry waves against the walls and cliffs, that rise to the world above …. We have an unknown distance yet to run; an unknown river yet to explore."

Nine men entered the canyon that day. But three soon concluded that the rapids were too difficult. Deciding to give up the trip, the three climbed to the rim of the canyon—and were quickly killed by Indians. Powell led the rest of his men safely through the canyon, which proved to be more than two hundred miles long.

In 1903, President Theodore Roosevelt, a strong supporter of parks, stood at the rim of the canyon. "Do nothing to mar its grandeur," he advised others, "…keep it for your children, your children's children, and all who come after you, as the one great sight which every American should see." But even the Grand Canyon had a rocky path to preservation. Tourists taking Roosevelt's advice flocked to the Arizona Territory to see it. The Santa Fe Railroad completed a spur line to the South Rim, and the grand El Tovar Hotel was erected. The canyon was designated a national monument in 1908, but mining interests fought park status and other men dreamed of building dams and irrigation projects utilizing the rushing waters of the Colorado. Congress finally approved a park bill for the Grand Canyon in 1919, but only after including assurances that existing land claims would not be affected and that power and reclamation projects could be approved by the Secretary of the Interior.

The American Southwest contains thousands of cliff dwellings and other sites where Native Americans lived long ago. As more and more modern-day Americans moved into the Southwest, vandalism and looting of these sites became a problem. Bowls and jewelry and other items could be resold to collectors, and greedy pot-hunters dug through the ruins. At the Cliff Palace, on Mesa Verde in southwestern Colorado, looters knocked down a wall with blasting powder.

Congress responded in 1906. First, Mesa Verde was made a national park. Second, the Antiquities Act, prohibiting individuals from damaging or removing any historic object from public lands, was signed into law. The act also permitted the president to create, by proclamation, "national monuments." This designation was to be used primarily to protect ancient sites. However, presidents have also proclaimed various forts, battlefields, canyons, and caves as national monuments. The Antiquities Act greatly increased the number of units in the park system, because the monuments did not require the approval of Congress. The prehistoric and historic units of the National Park System, although not the focus of this book, are equally important parts of the heritage of all Americans. Because of space limitations, this book cannot mention every unit of the system that preserves a natural area.

Devils Tower, in Wyoming, was the first national monument proclaimed by President Roosevelt, in 1906. This volcanic rock, resembling the stump of a tree, rises 865 feet above the plains. Most Americans would recognize Devils Tower as the spot where the alien spaceship landed in the motion picture *Close Encounters of the Third Kind.*

Lassen Peak, a volcanic mountain in northern California, was proclaimed a national monument in 1907. The volcano was thought to be extinct, but the experts were wrong! It erupted in 1914, and Congress wasted no time in upgrading Lassen to the status of a national park. At about the same time (1912), a powerful volcanic eruption dramatically altered the landscape in the Mount Katmai region in Alaska, and ultimately resulted (in 1980) in the creation of Katmai National Park and Preserve.

Although the story of the parks is one of continual growth in the amount of acreage given protection, there have been painful setbacks. Early in the twentieth century, a lovely part of Yosemite National Park was lost. The city of San Francisco promoted a plan to dam Hetch Hetchy Valley within the park in order to create a lake to augment its water supply.

Outraged, John Muir, Yosemite's leading defender, organized a national outcry, arguing that Hetch Hetchy Valley was comparable in beauty to nearby Yosemite Valley. But the last-ditch effort was doomed to defeat. Congress approved the dam in 1913, and a disheartened John Muir died shortly thereafter. Nonetheless, the cloud of defeat had a silver lining. This dispute was the first major confrontation between the budding conservation movement and Congress. Many individuals who had followed the debate concluded that it was important to protect the parks from any further damage.

By 1916 there were fourteen national parks and twenty-one national monuments. In that year, Congress approved the National Parks Organic Act, which stated that the purpose of the parks and monuments was "to conserve the scenery and the natural and historic objects and the wild life therein and … leave them unimpaired for the enjoyment of future generations." Toward that end, the law established a new agency, the National Park Service, to administer the newly designated National Park System.

Stephen T. Mather, a California businessman, had previously written Secretary of the Interior Franklin Lane to complain that the parks were in bad shape. Cattle were grazing inside the parks, and loggers were eager to cut some tall trees that were supposedly protected. Lane wrote back, "Dear Steve: If you don't like the way the national parks are run, why don't you come down to Washington and run them yourself."

Mather accepted the challenge, becoming the first director of the National Park Service. He had the ability to motivate idealistic young people who wanted to work in the outdoors and do their part to preserve America's natural heritage. He established a tradition of dedication and commitment to the parks that continues to this day. Mather, by the way, began with a total Park Service administrative budget of $19,500 a year, which included his own salary of $4,500.

Around the same time, concerned parks supporters founded the National Parks and Conservation Association in an effort to "defend the National Parks and Monuments fearlessly against assaults of private interests and aggressive commercialism."

That conditions were poor in the national parks no one could dispute. On the day that Horace Albright, Mather's assistant, inspected a shabby campground in Yellowstone run by fast-buck operators, twenty people there were stricken with ptomaine poisoning.

During World War I, the fledgling Park Service beat back proposals by food processors to slaughter buffalo and elk in Yellowstone. The processors had contended that the meat was needed for the war effort. In the noble cause of helping to make the world safe for democracy, a few sheep and cattle were allowed to munch on the wildflowers in two parks. During the war, the Park Service persuaded Congress to remove the Army from Yellowstone and give the NPS the opportunity to run the park with its own team of rangers. The era of the men and women in the green hats—so familiar and so admired now by millions of visitors—was under way.

After the war, the Park Service could look ahead to a period of rapid growth in the number of parks and monuments. The advent of the automobile, driven by tourists with more free time, foreshadowed a sharp increase in the popularity of the parks.

The national parks created so far were all west of the Mississippi River. Glacier and Rocky Mountain National Parks now crowned the crest of the continent, and Hawaii and Alaska each had a park. Most of the parks were of the "monumental" model, and all had been carved from the public domain. But the future would bring parks in the East, some of them smaller in size, some barely snatched from the encroachment of humanity, and some purchased with private or public funds.

In 1919 Lafayette (now Acadia) National Park in Maine became the first park east of the Mississippi River. Undertaking another one-man crusade that lasted for decades, George B. Dorr, a Bostonian and heir to a textile fortune, persuaded his wealthy neighbors on Mount Desert Island to donate land for the park. John D. Rockefeller, Jr., contributed eleven thousand acres, almost a third of the park. On the island, granite mountains rise from the sea and overlook a rugged, rocky shore that is pounded constantly by the waves of the Atlantic Ocean. Acadia is a dramatic example of nature in conflict with itself.

Other gifts of land or money helped create more parks. In 1926, Great Smoky Mountains (Tennessee, North Carolina), Shenandoah (Virginia), and Mammoth Cave (Kentucky) joined the honor roll of National Parks. John D. Rockefeller, Jr., again came to the rescue, giving $5 million to the government to buy land for the park in the Smokies. But thousands of average citizens also made donations. Schoolchildren collected pocket change to help save what was left of this virgin forest from the woodsman's blade. The wisdom of establishing parks in the populous East has been demonstrated many times; the Smoky Mountains park, for example, attracts far more visitors than either Yellowstone or Yosemite.

Florida's Everglades National Park, authorized in 1934, represented another new departure. This vast "river of grass"—derided by some as an ugly swamp—did not have the visual appeal of snow-capped mountains or green forests, but it did have the East's largest concentration of birds, including masses of graceful egrets, herons, and storks. The park, which also harbors alligators and crocodiles within its mudflats and ponds, was the first to be established primarily because of its wildlife resources.

Rockefeller, meanwhile, was the prime mover in the rescue of another sumptuous landscape. The Grand Tetons of Wyoming, viewed from the sagebrush flats to the east, are perhaps the most sublime mountain façade in the Rockies. They lie within the public domain, and the creation of a small Grand Teton National Park in 1926, limited mostly to the mountains themselves, was no problem. What sends their scenic index off the charts is Jackson Hole, the capacious, open valley of the meandering Snake River, which lies at the base of the thirteen thousand-foot spires. By the 1920s, the valley was being checkerboarded with gas stations and billboards. Horace Albright, superintendent at Yellowstone, escorted Rockefeller to Jackson Hole in 1926, and chose a vantage point that required the multimillionaire to peer at the enchanted mountains through a cluster of telephone poles. Rockefeller, though no stranger to private enterprise, was offended by the old dance hall, dilapidated cabins, and other entrepreneurial detritus that spoiled his view. He subsequently agreed to organize the Snake River Land Company, with his own name carefully kept secret (to prevent speculators from driving up prices), and it proceeded to buy up private land in Jackson Hole. By 1933, Rockefeller had spent $1.4 million for 35,000 acres.

When the truth came out, local ranchers and homesteaders, hard-hit by the Great Depression, were embittered by the infusion of East Coast wealth to buy their valley. Wyoming political leaders fought for years to prevent the transfer of Rockefeller's purchases for an expanded park. Finally, in 1950, twenty-four years after committing his resources to a grander Grand Teton Park, Rockefeller could celebrate the addition of Jackson Hole—or most of it—to the park.

The World War II years were quiet ones in the parks, but postwar prosperity brought a new rush of tourists. With the passing decades, visitors had an ever-growing menu of landscapes and seascapes on which to feast their eyes. In Washington state, Mount Olympus and its attendant dripping forests and surf-lashed seashore had become a national park. The haunting cry of a loon at night on a Minnesota lake was preserved for posterity at Voyageurs National Park. The Kodachrome canyon country of southern and eastern Utah, endless twisting avenues of red, white, pink, and orange rock, now contained no fewer than five national parks. Joshua Tree, Saguaro, and Organ Pipe Cactus National Monuments protected bizarre plants and ecosystems that only the low hot desert seemed able to harbor.

With the growth of the park system came growing pains. In the 1950s, the dam builders and the environmental movement squared off for a second time. Early in the century, public protests had failed to prevent the construction of a reservoir in Hetch Hetchy Valley inside Yosemite National Park. Now, the federal government had its eye on a little-known (to the general public) region in the upper drainage basin of the Colorado River.

Dinosaur National Monument, straddling Utah and Colorado, contains an awesome collection of dinosaur bones. The spines, legbones, and neckbones of the huge reptiles had piled up on a sandbar of a river millions of years ago. Erosion of the land has revealed the bones.

The monument also includes deep canyons of the Green and Yampa rivers. Ever on the lookout for new sources for hydropower, the U.S. Bureau of Reclamation, another agency within the Interior Department, proposed to build a dam at Echo Park, inside the monument.

By this time, however, the environmental movement was much bigger—and better prepared, too. David Brower, executive director of the Sierra Club, testified that assertions made on behalf of the dam were incorrect. Through the use of scientific studies, Brower demonstrated that the high evaporation rate of the impounded water would make the dam's construction much more expensive than the government had claimed.

In opposing the bill to build the Echo Park Dam, Senator Paul Douglas of Illinois warned that construction of such a reservoir would help transform the country "into a placid, tepid place, greatly unlike the wild and stirring America which we love and from which

we draw inspiration." Ultimately, proponents of the dam abandoned the fight in the face of reason and public pressure. The bill before Congress was revised to exclude the Dinosaur dam.

But even in victory, the environmentalists suffered a defeat. The same bill provided for the flooding of the Glen Canyon on the Colorado River in southern Utah. Although the scenery here was lovely, it had not been added to the National Park System. Glen Canyon, so named by Major Powell in 1869, was a secluded world where birdsongs resonated in vaulted stone chambers, waterfalls tinkled into shadowed plunge pools, and the river itself flowed gently, as if resting before it entered the *sturm und drang* of the Grand Canyon. The Glen Canyon that challenged Powell's literary talents survives only in the fading inks and dyes of *The Place No One Knew: Glen Canyon on the Colorado*, a book of Eliot Porter's photographs, an elegy for a lost world published by the Sierra Club.

Ironically, Lake Powell, the reservoir created by the dam, did become a part of the park system as Glen Canyon National Recreation Area. Many visitors who plow across the lake in motorboats today find the lake and its setting exhilarating, but they do not know what was drowned beneath the water, and they may have difficulty accepting that the dead waters have backed up underneath Rainbow Bridge, arguably the world's most beautiful rock formation—and yet another unit in the park system.

Nonetheless, with the defeat of the attempt to build a dam in Dinosaur National Monument, preservationists could claim that they had established the principle that no dams would deface the parks. Right? Wrong! Another painful lesson had yet to be learned: No victories are ever final! Battles that have been "won" may need to be refought by the next generation. And once a particular battle has been lost—once the outstanding feature of a park has been dammed, paved over, or otherwise damaged—the park almost never can be restored to its original beauty.

The law that made the Grand Canyon a national park in 1919 contained a clause that left open the possibility that dams could be constructed within the gorge. In

1963, the government announced that two dams would be built in the canyon as part of a broad plan to overcome the water shortage in the Southwest, where cities like Phoenix and Las Vegas were booming. The dams would flood 146 miles of the Colorado River inside the canyon. Behind the dams, the foaming river that had been carving the gorge for eons of time would fall silent and still.

David Brower of the Sierra Club took out full-page newspaper ads in 1966. One said, in part, "… there is only one simple, incredible issue here: this time it's the Grand Canyon they want to flood. The Grand Canyon!" Advocates of the dam argued that the reservoir would hardly be visible from the canyon rims, a mile or more above. Bureau of Reclamation director Floyd Dominy pointed out that visitors could travel easily on the lake to examine the billion-year-old rocks up close. Of course, the lake would eliminate one of the world's supreme wilderness adventures, a float trip through the canyon's many whitewater rapids. Another Sierra Club ad posed this question: "Should we also flood the Sistine Chapel so tourists can get nearer the ceiling?"

Charged by the Internal Revenue Service with attempting "substantially" to influence legislation, the Sierra Club was stripped of its tax-exempt status, tripled its membership in two years, and won its fight. When it came time to twist senatorial arms in Capitol cloakrooms, defenders of the Grand Canyon pointed out that the dams would serve only as cash registers, and that hydroelectric power generated by the dams would be sold to finance the construction of water development elsewhere. Other sources, they demonstrated, could provide electric power at less cost. A blizzard of letters to Congress denounced the dams. Convinced that they were right and knowing that the public was behind them, the conservationists refused to compromise. Neither dam was built.

In 1961, the U.S. government established a precedent by spending $16 million of the taxpayers' money to purchase the land for Cape Cod National Seashore in Massachusetts. That amount, however, was a pittance compared with the cost for Redwood National Park in California. The coast redwood trees are the world's tallest living things—not to be confused with their woody cousins, the sequoias, in the Sierra Nevada, which are the world's most massive living objects. Through the efforts of John Muir and his disciples, the greatest stands of the Sierran forests had been protected in national parks established in 1890. But the redwoods, flourishing amid the fog and moisture of the northern California coast, were mostly in the possession of logging companies who saw in them fine pieces of furniture. The clear-cutting of virgin redwoods accelerated beyond the rate of one million board feet per year in the 1950s. The Save-the-Redwoods League, later joined by the Sierra Club, worked tirelessly for decades to save the trees, and the Muir Woods National Monument (1908) and several state parks were established to preserve several parcels of forest.

A survey released in 1964 showed that 85 percent of the primeval redwoods had already fallen. Congress acted to bring 58,000 acres into a Redwood National Park in 1968 that included a "legislative taking" of private land. Benefits to be paid to loggers who lost their jobs were projected at $100 million, and the overall cost, including the purchase of 48,000 more acres in 1978, approached the $1 billion mark.

In the late 1970s the National Park System comprised about three hundred units containing some thirty million acres. During that period, the addition of only a few more parks and monuments more than doubled the acreage of the system. Late in the twentieth century, this dramatic expansion could have occurred in only one state: Alaska. The nation's largest state, more than twice the size of Texas, Alaska was also by far the wildest and least populated. Relatively few Americans were hardy enough or sufficiently dedicated to accept Alaska on its own harsh terms.

Before statehood (1959) the federal government owned 99 percent of Alaska, and the state was admitted to the Union with the understanding that it would get 100 million acres (out of a total of 375 million). The native Alaskans—Inuits (Eskimos), Aleuts, and Indians—also asserted claims for land. In 1971, Congress agreed to give the natives 44 million acres and nearly $1 billion. Thanks to the efforts of Dr. Edgar Wayburn of the

Sierra Club and many other environmentalists, that law also provided that the government study up to 80 million acres for possible inclusion in the national parks, national forests, and national wildlife refuges. Complex negotiations got under way, with the natives and the development-minded state politicians battling with the federal government over which lands they would control and which lands would go to the parks.

In 1978, with the deadline at hand for Congress to implement the clause in the 1971 law that authorized new parks, and with no agreement in sight, President Jimmy Carter used his authority to create national monuments, thus protecting the scenery-rich landscapes until the final park boundaries could be drawn. That was accomplished in 1980. Ronald Reagan, who was unsympathetic to the preservationists' dreams for maximum Alaskan parklands, had just been elected president.

Therefore, in the subsequent lame-duck session of Congress preceding Reagan's inauguration, the House settled for a compromise Senate bill that was less protective than the House majority had wanted.

Nonetheless, what additions had been made to the "crown jewels," and what new meaning had been given to that description! Denali National Park was tripled in size to six million acres. Its crowning glory, Mount McKinley, the top of the continent, splits the sky eighteen thousand feet above its base, at an altitude of 20,320 feet. The seashore mountains of Wrangell-St. Elias shrink human contrivances to near-invisibility, and whole states of people could be hidden within the park's 13.2 million empty acres. In Lake Clark National Park and Preserve, smoking volcanoes riding on restless tectonic plates promise more conflict between the forces of fire and ice. The permanently frozen ground and howling wilderness of Gates of the Arctic National Park and Preserve provide the ultimate test of our resourcefulness as matched against the uncaring laws of nature.

Altogether, eight areas in Alaska bear the designation "park" or "park and preserve." The great achievement in Alaska is that entire river basins and mountain ranges have been preserved. Migration routes of animal herds have been protected. Mistakes made in the allocation of park acreage in the "Lower Forty-Eight" have by and large been avoided in Alaska. If Alaska is the Last Frontier, as its boosters call it, it may also be the last best hope on Earth for survival of what is left of nature's kingdom.

The National Park System of 1994 embraces nearly 375 units, with more than half of them classified as historical. At 0.02 acres, Thaddeus Kosciuszko National Memorial in Philadelphia is the antithesis of Wrangell-St. Elias. Some 80 million acres are distributed across forty-nine states (Delaware is the exception), the District of Columbia, American Samoa, Puerto Rico, the Virgin Islands, Guam, and Saipan. Annual visits approach 300 million. The units fall into twenty-three categories, including such fine distinctions as national rivers and national wild and scenic riverways. There is one national mall (in the District of Columbia) and the White House, which is in a classification by itself. National forests and national wildlife refuges are not part of the National Park System.

Superimposed on this jargon jungle is another kind of classification: wilderness. The Wilderness Act of 1964, the goal of The Wilderness Society for a generation, designates areas in the United States where "there shall be no commercial enterprise and no permanent road … no use of motor vehicles, motorized equipment or motor boats, no landing of aircraft, no other form of mechanical transport, and no structure or installation." Those who make a living extracting minerals from the ground or letting livestock graze upon it were aghast at the idea of "locking up" vast tracts of land as wilderness. But proponents did not visualize setting aside more than a small percentage of the American landscape as wilderness. The effect of the Wilderness Act on the parks was that of creating zones, one in which no motorized activity was permitted, and one in which a greater variety of recreation was allowed. Not all the wilderness was to be drawn from National Park Service lands; acreage administered by the U.S. Forest Service, Fish and Wildlife Service, and Bureau of Land Management was also to be considered for such protection.

The process of evaluating and designating wilderness areas continues today, with "special interests" fighting state-by-state to keep the wilderness areas as small in size and number as possible. But public sentiment runs strongly in favor of wilderness. Millions of Americans whose recreational pursuits do not include backpacking and canoeing simply want to know that untouched country still exists, perhaps even idyllic places where lions lay down with lambs, and mysterious places are populated with water sprites and trolls.

However, only a minority of the visitors to the parks are actually seeking wilderness. On a typical summer weekend, more than fifty thousand visitors park their campers or pitch their tents in the 450 campgrounds administered by the Park Service, and the recreational vehicles appear to far outnumber the tents. True wilderness buffs are not found in the campgrounds, and they don't hang out in places like "Yosemite Village." The upper portion of Yosemite Valley has long resembled a small town, featuring at one time or another tennis courts, a pitch-and-putt golf course, a bank, a delicatessen, a skating rink, three swimming pools, a barber shop, a beauty shop, thirty-three kennels, and thirteen package liquor stores.

The Park Service went through a period in which somewhat unnatural entertainment was provided for visitors. Both the Yellowstone Act of 1872 and the National Park Service Act of 1916 had said that the parks must not only preserve nature but also provide enjoyment for visitors. Early directors, eager to build rapidly a constituency in support of the national park concept, fostered the entertainment aspect. Grandstands were built at Yellowstone to provide a good view of bears being fed garbage. Other animals were chained near the hotels. Floodlights illuminated Old Faithful at night. In Yosemite Valley, logs and bark were set on fire and pushed off 3,000-foot-high Glacier Point at night to thrill visitors. The grandeur of nature was reduced to serving as a source of cheap amusement, and those Yellowstone bears became beggars that sometimes even attacked visitors.

Today, swimming pools and animal exhibitions are out, and the official policy is that animals take precedence over people. There is less human effort to control wildlife populations, and age-old predator-prey relationships are being restored where possible.

As a footnote to all this, it should be noted that the government has received plenty of free advice about how to entertain visitors. In 1923, when the town of Shelby, Montana, had a surplus of natural gas and Glacier National Park had no volcanoes (it still doesn't have any), a plan was floated to pipe the gas sixty miles to Chief Mountain within the park, where it would serve to create eruptions that, according to one article, would "rival Vesuvius or any of the other Old World 'smokers.' " The most serious threats to the parks are the most subtle ones, and they are revealed in the slow degradation of the park experience. Pollution from power plants and coastal cities has gradually reduced the broad crystal-clear vistas in the open country of the West. In the East, an unnatural, man-made haze mixes with the natural blue haze that gives the Smokies their name. Throughout the country, even in Acadia National Park in Maine, far distant from major population centers, sulfur-laden acid rain is killing forests as well as the inhabitants of ponds and lakes. Streams flowing through parks carry sewage and pesticides that poison wildlife. In the Grand Canyon, wilderness campers and hikers were distracted by the buzzing of fifty thousand sight-seeing overflights a year by helicopters and small planes, many of which swooped below the canyon rims. It took a mid-air collision of two planes that killed twenty-five people over the canyon in 1986 to spur Congress to reduce the number of overflights. Competing preferences of visitors must be weighed, with a compromise that fails to satisfy anybody the almost certain result.

In its 1980 State of the Parks report to Congress, the National Park Service declared Glacier National Park to be the most endangered park in the system. The National Parks and Conservation Association, examining the park eight years later, found little improvement. Aside from the usual documented troubles—poaching, livestock wandering onto park land, air pollution, and helicopter overflights—Glacier had special problems, too, many of them shared with other parks as well. Clear-cutting along park borders constituted not only an eyesore but a threat to wildlife that migrated in and out of the park. Oil companies, searching for oil and gas preserves, detonated explosives right up to the park boundaries, shattering the solitude of wilderness explorers. Prospective mining in Canada would pollute the North Fork of the Flathead River upstream of the park. The suppression of naturally caused fires carried with it the threat of uncontrollable blazes in the future.

The conservationist Aldo Leopold wrote that across the vast prairie of the Midwest the tall grass once tickled the bellies of millions of buffalo. Most of the buffalo are gone, and the same must be said of the bluestem and other grasses that once covered 400,000 square miles. But in Kansas and Oklahoma, fragments of the tallgrass prairie still survive, where the windblown fields roll like ocean waves in a stiff breeze. If the terms of purchase can be worked out, a Tallgrass Prairie National Preserve will join our roster of parks.

The consideration of other potential future parks, those having national rather than regional significance, continues. No one is likely to discover another Yosemite Valley, but Congress is considering a Mojave National Park in California that would preserve the threatened desert lying within a short jaunt of millions of people. The Big Sur section of the California coastline deserves to be included, and the same holds true for Anasazi ruins and rock art of the Southwest. The San Rafael Swell, a bizarre broken country of naked sandstone in eastern Utah, must have protection to survive threats from mining and off-road vehicles. The Florida Keys and the Columbia River Gorge cry out for additional protection.

The distinguished writer Wallace Stegner observed, "No other nation on Earth so swiftly wasted its birthright; no other, in time, made such an effort to save what was left." Perhaps hearing the yet-unspoken pleas of descendants that they would never know, certainly mindful of a nearly defenseless natural world, much of which they would never see, enough Americans came forward to say, "these parks we must preserve." In coming to the rescue of the natural world, man symbolically rejoined it.

In Acadia National Park, Maine, the 1858 Bass Harbor Head Light stands guard over rugged granite cliffs, which are often subjected to fierce pounding by the storm-tossed Atlantic Ocean.

THE EAST

In the continental United States the day begins in Maine, and in Acadia National Park it very often emerges from a seamless white fog. Yielding to the burning power of a rising but yet unseen sun, the fog draws back slowly, affording a wondrous sight, conjuring before your eyes the primal Creation of Genesis. From where you stand, an ever-broader and sloping shelf of boulders—jagged, slippery, aimlessly tossed yet curiously sorted by size, and strewn with kelp—comes into view.

Beyond the "rockbound coast" you can now see an ever-larger expanse of water, not alive yet never still, heedless of time yet syn-

On Acadia's rocky shore, the tide rises and falls constantly, tossing up detritus from the ocean and providing frequent surprises for beachcombers.

The summit of Cadillac Mountain, the highest point on the eastern coast, is the first place in the United States to catch the rays of the rising sun. At dawn, visitors to Acadia gather on the mountaintop to welcome the new day.

chronized precisely with movements of the sun and moon, allowing calculations of the tides to the minute. Up from the beach, the parting mists reveal scrubby vegetation surrounding a quiet lily pond occupied by waterfowl. Finally, in the east, a strange pale sun appears, above an assumed horizon in a still-invisible sky. Perhaps only by mid-morning is a conventional world fully in place, vast in scale under a blue bowl painted with soaring gulls and bordered by carpets of conifers thrown over granite mountains.

Acadia occupies most of Mount Desert Island, which was largely formed hundreds of millions of years ago by the upwelling of magma from deep in the earth, then scoured by glaciers within the past eighteen thousand years. Today another force, the Atlantic Ocean, tears at the stone fortress. From the peak of Cadillac Mountain, 1,530 feet, highest on the eastern seaboard, one can see islands that were part of the mainland until the ocean, rising with melted ice, surrounded them.

Along the coast, in the intertidal zones exposed only at low or intermediate tides, many plants and animals flourish in spite of assaults of the sea. Marine snails called periwinkles graze on the blue-green alga, which has stained the rocks black. Millions of acorn barnacles cling to the rocks. The rubbery rockweed, anchored to the rocks by tentacles called holdfasts, lies flat when exposed but floats upright underwater. Further down, in zones exposed only rarely during low tides, crabs, sea stars, and sea urchins settle in among the Irish moss and kelp. At sea, porpoises, seals, and five species of whales consume fish, squid, and other ocean creatures.

With all the scattered villages and inholdings, Mount Desert Island and the park are less than a wilderness. But the cycle of nature, first forceful, then serene, is dominant.

Some 120 miles northwest of Acadia, Mount Katahdin rises 5,267 feet above the lay of the land, the highest point in Maine, the centerpiece of Baxter State Park, and northern terminus for the 2,100-mile Appalachian National Scenic Trail. Constructed by volunteers from 1922 to 1927, the trail has welcomed uncounted thousands of visitors who have hiked a portion of it, as well as an energetic few who have walked its entire length.

The Appalachian Mountains in Shenandoah National Park are ancient even as mountain ridges go, and their peaks have been rounded by many millions of years of erosion.

From the crest of the Blue Ridge, traversed by the famous Skyline Drive through Shenandoah National Park, visitors can look down into the historic Shenandoah Valley, a route taken by both early settlers and Civil War troops.

The sun's brilliance is softened by the pervasive haze that puts the "blue" in the Blue Ridge. Many hiking trails in Shenandoah lead downward from the Skyline Drive.

For those who attempt the entire distance at one time, months are required, and the usual approach is to begin in April at the southern terminus, Springer Mountain in Georgia, and follow the changing seasons north. Through fourteen states, the trail follows the dominant topographic feature of the East, the Appalachian Mountains—really a nearly continuous chain of individual ranges, including the Great Smokies, the Blue Ridge, Lehigh and South mountains, the Catskills, and the Taconic, White, and Green mountains of New England. As mountains go, the Appalachians are quite old, and erosion—the great leveler—has worn down and rounded off the system's numberless peaks.

Rich in coal, iron ore, marble, and granite, Appalachia is nonetheless the home of many impoverished people, abandoned along with emptied quarries and strip-mined land when corporations and entrepreneurs moved their operations elsewhere. Tourism has brought a lift to some parts of the mountain region, as millions of residents of the crowded East seek refuge in the state and federal recreation areas in the high country, including Great Smoky Mountains and Shenandoah national parks. The Appalachian Trail meanders through these parks, but far more Americans gain access to them through a paved trail more suited to four wheels than two feet.

The town of Front Royal, Virginia, in an apple-growing region sixty miles west of Washington, D.C., is the jumping-off place for perhaps the longest automobile odyssey in the park system, and

Great Smoky Mountains National Park, in North Carolina and Tennessee, contains the largest remaining virgin forest in the eastern United States. More people visit the Smokies each year than any other park.

one of the most appealing. Just south of Front Royal, a left turn brings motorists onto Skyline Drive and into Shenandoah National Park. For 105 miles to the southwest through the pencil-shaped park, the drive follows the crest of the range. (Contrary to the song's lyrics— "In the Blue Ridge Mountains of Virginia/On the trail of the lonesome pine"—it's just called the Blue Ridge.) The Skyline Drive is so famous in itself that many people traverse it without realizing that they are also in a park called Shenandoah.

The Blue Ridge here forms the eastern rampart of the Appalachians. The metamorphic and igneous rock is as much as one billion years old; to the west, the looping Shenandoah River is visible for the length of the park. South of where the river splits into its northern and southern forks, massive Massanutten Mountain rises within the valley itself.

In 1926, by the time the park was authorized, many settlers on the ridge had migrated elsewhere in search of a better living, and the government subsequently bought out or resettled the rest. A forest of oak, hickory, and a hundred other species now spreads across 95 percent of the park, and indeed two-fifths of the park has been designated a wilderness area. Deer, bears, bobcats, and turkeys, once missing or rare, have returned. Trails lead steeply down the sides of the ridge, alive in the spring with banks of pink azaleas and mountain laurel and cascades of water. Fall foliage is brilliant, and open winter vistas from the ridge lift the spirits.

The highway, after dropping into Rockfish Gap near Waynesboro, exits the park and metamorphoses into the Blue Ridge Parkway, a unit in the National Park System by that name. For 469 miles, in Virginia and North Carolina, the road passes along some of the grandest mountain scenery in the eastern United States at an average altitude of three thousand feet. Turnouts provide panorama after panorama of craggy mountains and haze-dimmed valleys.

The rusticity of the Blue Ridge is tied a great deal to the preserved homesteads of the old-timers who once lived here, operating moonshine stills and all too often communicating with their neighbors through exchanges of shotgun blasts. Split-rail fences, log cabins, and old gristmills are part of the charm of the Blue Ridge country. Mount Mitchell, the highest mountain east of the Mississippi River at an elevation of 6,684 feet, rises just to the west of the parkway in North Carolina.

More than four hundred bears roam the Smokies. Most bears, on hearing or smelling hikers, prefer to slip away unseen, but occasionally a mother protecting her cubs will attack humans.

Congaree Swamp National Monument, in South Carolina, embraces ninety species of trees—half as many as in all of Europe. Eight kinds of woodpeckers, including the rare red-cockaded woodpecker, live within the dense riverbottom hardwood forest.

Cades Cove is a broad valley, six miles long, inside Great Smoky Mountains National Park. The mill, cabins, churches, and large pastures with grazing horses preserve the rural, nineteenth-century character of the cove.

The parkway terminates at the southern entrance to Great Smoky Mountains National Park. The Smokies are the culmination of the Southern Appalachians, and from vantage points they roll away to the horizon, tier after tier.

Clouds moving in from the west are pushed up by the mountains and release their moisture. Into each life, it is said, some rain must fall, and the prolific life of the Smokies relies on a great deal of precipitation, which can be snowflakes in the highlands and drizzle in the lowlands, simultaneously. Fog smothers the forest in the morning, and the sight and sound of numerous cascades and swift streams add to the pervasive sense of dampness.

The precipitation and the fertile soil together have created a world-renowned flora—1,400 kinds of flowering plants, 130 trees, 230 lichens, almost 300 mosses and liverworts, and at least 2,000 fungi. Trees are everywhere, blanketing almost the entire park. Higher elevations feature the red spruce more familiar to Maine and Canada. Beeches, maples, birches, and buckeyes occupy the middle slope—their turning leaves a visual treat in autumn. The southern hardwood forests are loveliest in spring, when flowering dogwoods and silver bells blossom.

Red, white, and pink rhododendrons crowd the summits and slopes in summer while trillium, spring beauties, bluets, and trout lilies flood the forest floor in the spring. This great mass of plant life, rarely equaled in temperate zones worldwide, exudes the hydrocarbons and water vapor that form the highlands' filmy haze, or "smoke."

The most frequently encountered representative of the animal kingdom is *Homo sapiens*, and more than eight million of them can be seen in the park each year. Indeed, the Great Smokies is the park most often visited by this species. Because the woods are so dense, and because many human visitors stay inside or near their metal carapaces, they can easily be avoided by hikers who venture onto the nine hundred miles of trails. In the woods, with luck, black bears may be sighted frequently. Bears have the good sense to sleep through the winter, and hairless eight-ounce cubs, usually two in number, are born in January while mother dozes away, often in a hollow tree. By March, the furred cubs and their mother are ready to join, or rejoin, the world.

Water, in the form of precipitation, creates the beauty of the Great Smokies, and direct interactions between land and water are responsible for other unique and protected environments of the East.

Everglades National Park, at the southern tip of the Florida mainland, is the largest eastern park, but it may not be large enough to survive, and indeed Everglades may become an extinct park as the natural systems outside and within the preserve decline to the point where the park can no longer sustain its resident wildlife. The park cannot be described or discussed in isolation from the fact of its decline.

The Everglades has been called a river of grass, but the river is most unusual— six inches deep, fifty miles wide, one hundred miles long. Water advances generally southward toward the Bay of Florida in a broad shallow sheet at the rate of one-half mile per day, on a gradient of two or three inches per mile. The river is underlain with limestone, which supports the sawgrass that occupies it. The land is so flat that the highest points of ground—one at an elevation of twenty feet—are piles of shells discarded by the indigenous peoples of many centuries ago. Islands called hammocks rise one to three feet above the limestone and support hardwoods that include live oak, mahogany, and strangler fig. Thick stands of mangroves crowd the coast, where salt water and fresh water mix.

This, the largest subtropical wilderness in the contiguous United States, is home to alligators, crocodiles, panthers, and a world-renowned assemblage of wading birds. But no more than thirty

This lighthouse, on Cape Hatteras National Seashore, is the tallest in the United States at 208 feet. Just beyond these Outer Banks lies the "Graveyard of the Atlantic," where six hundred ships have been wrecked, victims of shallow shoals, storms, and wars.

panthers survive in the "glades" and in the Big Cypress Preserve to the north. Crocodiles are rare, too. The waders have declined by 90 percent since the 1930s, though they still gather in impressive numbers in drying pools in winter to harvest fish, frogs, and other edible creatures.

The boom in human population in south Florida has placed a heavy strain on the water supply and on other species that depend on its unobstructed movement. The watershed for the Everglades is 240 miles to the north. But in the 1940s, the U.S. Army Corps of Engineers began to channelize the Kissimmee River and send its flow into Lake Okeechobee. In turn that water was removed from the lake, to supply the needs of agriculture as well as Miami and other cities, by means of a complex of canals, dikes, and levees. The supply of water to the Everglades fell sharply. As the fish declined in number, wading birds stopped nesting. Rather than see their young starve, for example, resident wood storks declined to nest for several consecutive years in the 1980s. Even the gentle manatees, or sea cows, that swim the waters of Florida Bay are being thinned by bloody encounters with the propellers of motorboats.

Many Floridians are working tirelessly to prevent the demise of the park. In the early 1990s, acreage was added to the park, and a costly plan was worked out with the federal government and with sugar growers and other large farming concerns to restore some of the natural flow of the river and filter some pollutants contained in agricultural runoffs.

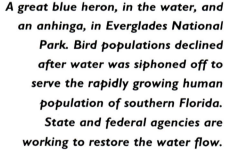

A great blue heron, in the water, and an anhinga, in Everglades National Park. Bird populations declined after water was siphoned off to serve the rapidly growing human population of southern Florida. State and federal agencies are working to restore the water flow.

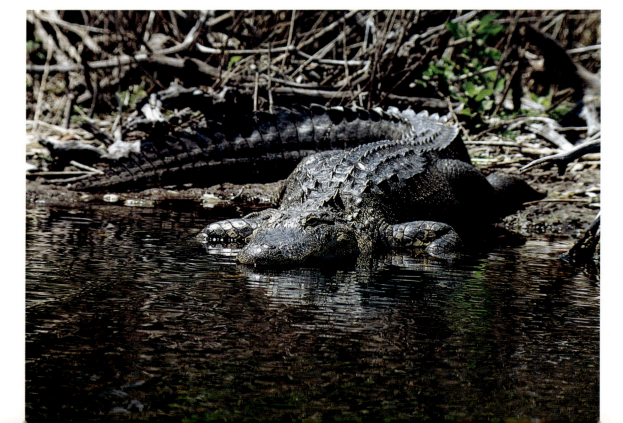

Alligators in the Everglades conserve energy by basking in the sun for long periods of time without moving. When hungry, they strike at birds, turtles, raccoons, and even dogs and white-tailed deer. Humans dare not approach them.

In 1992, the Everglades took a frightful pounding from Hurricane Andrew, which toppled up to 30 percent of the park's pine trees. But all of the glades' panthers and most of the birds apparently survived the "storm of the century."

Twenty-one miles east of Everglades, Biscayne National Park, 95 percent underwater, occupies a short strip of mangrove-choked mainland, most of Biscayne Bay, a string of more than forty low islands, or keys, and a stretch of open sea. Early in the century pollutants were poisoning the portion of Biscayne Bay nearest to Miami, but the bay is recovering well. Indeed, the southern section is nearly pristine.

Biscayne is for snorkelers who swim past the coral reefs, underground rock fortresses up to one hundred feet high. The reefs are the work of millions of small animals called polyps, who have the magical ability to take chemicals from the sea and convert them to stone. As the polyps harden and become a permanent part of the reef, new generations grow atop the old. Nature's wildest indulgences are displayed here. Corals may take the form of deer antlers or the corrugated surface of the human brain.

Among the reefs swim fish of brilliant iridescent colors. Many move in schools, but the

Birds gather in large numbers in pools just after dawn in the Everglades, waiting quietly to capture passing fish with their long beaks.

*Following page:
Some people who have never been to Everglades National Park believe it to be a mysterious and dangerous place occupied by strange creatures. At a mist-dappled sunrise, the glades do indeed take on an ethereal mood.*

With Long Island at its back, the thirty-two-mile strip of land named Fire Island absorbs the full force of Atlantic Ocean storms. Isolated and deserted in winter, the national seashore attracts throngs of visitors and summer residents, mostly from New York City, during the warm months.

Cape Cod, in Massachusetts, is a glacial deposit that is constantly on the move as winds and water push the sand along the shorelines. On a long, hooked arm of land surrounded by the sea, hikers, cyclists, horseback riders, and fishermen enjoy the national seashore's endless beaches.

queen angelfish, bright blue and yellow, passes with deliberate grace. In waters where pirates once prowled, the most sinister inhabitants today are octopuses, eels, hammerhead sharks, and stingrays.

Water is also the catalyst for America's tropical paradise, the Caribbean island of St. John in the U.S. Virgin Islands. Virgin Islands National Park, though small as parks go, is rich in species of plant and animal life. Born of volcanic action, the home long ago of warlike Carib Indians and later of Danish sugar plantation masters and their black slaves, the islands today show little evidence of their tempestuous past. The forest of St. John, once leveled to make room for sugar cane and cotton, has regrown and, if not precisely of its original composition, it is sufficiently jungle-like to suit back-country hikers.

If Columbus, who discovered the islands in 1493 and named them for St. Ursula and her virgin companions, were to return today, he would still find quiet coves, limpid blue-green waters, and white sandy beaches fringed by lush green hills. In the low, dry southeastern part of St. John, cactus and other desert plants replace the dense growth of the higher elevations.

Bats, the only native mammals, scoop bothersome insects out of the air. Mongooses, donkeys, and

Horn Island, Mississippi, part of Gulf Islands National Seashore, is accessible only by boat. Primitive camping is permitted on the beaches, which are covered with brilliant white sand.

Padre Island extends for eighty miles along the Gulf Coast of Texas. Bird-watching and hunting for shells and other treasures of the sea are popular pastimes. Rattlesnakes live on the island, too.

Royal terns commandeer a beach in Cumberland Island National Seashore, along Georgia's Atlantic Coast. More than three hundred species of birds have been seen on the island, which is accessible only by boat.

Frozen Niagara is one of the beautifully sculptured formations in Kentucky's Mammoth Cave National Park. More than three hundred miles of passages have been explored in the world's longest cave system. Underground rivers flow through some deep chambers.

Most of Biscayne National Park, in Florida, consists of seawater and enchanting coral reefs. Most of the corals look like plants, but each is a colony of thousands of tiny animals, called polyps. Rock beauty fish, seen here, are among two hundred species that swim through Biscayne's reefs.

goats, all introduced species, eat some park resources. Lizards are everywhere. Geckos, snakes, and iguanas may cross your trail, not to mention an army of hermit crabs moving through the uplands. The abundant bird life ranges from pelicans to hummingbirds and cuckoos. The white beaches—Trunk Bay is considered one of the world's ten best—are formed from particles of hard coral, smashed to bits by storm-tossed waves. Snorkelers can hear parrotfish chewing on the reef and grunts grunting, and can swim past the curious trunkfish as it spits a stream of water into the sand to uncover prey.

Buck Island Reef National Monument, only one-and-a-half miles from St. Croix, largest of the Virgin Islands, is another destination for snorkelers. Frigate birds glide for hours, riding the currents over the island and its submerged reef that teems with marine life.

Along the eastern seaboard of the U.S. mainland, at the interface between ocean and land, seven national seashores preserve fragments of the coast as it (approximately) was at the time seafaring explorers and the first early settlers sailed past in the 1600s.

Most of the seashores are barrier islands, long strips of sand paralleling the mainland, and they take a fierce pounding from both nature and man. Storms and occasional hurricanes flog the

beaches, rearranging the sand dunes and damaging or even destroying property, often astonishing vacation-home owners who, one gathers, were naive enough to buy land on the basis of slick brochures with picture-postcard views of serene and sunny seascapes. But the Atlantic is not a pacific ocean, and when nature bestirs itself we can be forcibly educated on its fury and caprice. Most of the Outer Banks of North Carolina are now part of Cape Hatteras and Cape Lookout National Seashores. The treacherous waters off the coast of the Outer Banks—the "Graveyard of the Atlantic"—have claimed more than six hundred ships. Storms sometimes uncover the ruins of old wrecks buried on the beaches.

The eastern beaches must also endure water polluted by medical waste, oil spills, and garbage discharged from ships. Offshore oil and gas development is a threat, and off-road vehicles chew up the dunes and obliterate fragile plants that help anchor the sand.

America's four national lakeshores are all found along the shores of the Great Lakes. These are gentler places as a rule, though towering dunes of glacial till and scoured bedrock are reminders of the force with which glaciers carved the lakes thousands of years ago.

The lake country is also home to two national parks. Isle Royale National Park occupies an island

Cinnamon Bay in Virgin Islands National Park. America's tropical paradise also includes relics of the Carib Indian civilization and historic Danish sugar plantations. Sailing, diving, snorkeling, and wind surfing entice the energetic.

forty-five miles long and nine miles wide in Lake Superior. The park, 99 percent wilderness, contains 166 miles of hiking trails and access is by boat and float plane only. Visibly, dramatically scraped by glaciers of immense weight, the island's volcanic rock slowly emerged as the level of the lake fell. Soil then developed, and plants and animals moved in. Today, the deep forests and small inland lakes provide one of the most secluded wilderness experiences in the contiguous U.S. In a recent year, only thirteen thousand visits were recorded on Isle Royale, the largest island in the largest freshwater lake in the world.

Moose swam to the island from Canada early in the century and proceeded to consume all of their food supply. Their numbers crashed, then recovered after a 1936 fire cleared the way for the regrowth of "moose salad." Eastern timber wolves crossed from the mainland on an ice bridge in the winter of 1948-1949, and proceeded to do the moose the considerable favor of culling their ranks of the old and ill. The rest of the moose stayed within their food supply and flourished. Sooner or later, however, it is the fate of almost every moose to perish in an assault by one of the highly organized and disciplined wolf packs. Biologists have studied the wolf-moose relationship since 1958, and sev-

Delaware National Scenic River, within Delaware Water Gap National Recreation Area, is one of the East's most popular canoe routes. The river, which runs along a thinly populated stretch not far from large cities, divides Pennsylvania and New Jersey.

eral books and many reports and articles have been the result. The numbers of predator and prey continue to rise and fall in relationship to each other.

One of Minnesota's nicknames is The Land of Ten Thousand Lakes, and thirty of them are within Voyageurs National Park along the Canadian border. Four times within the last million years—and as recently as eleven thousand years ago—massive ice sheets up to two miles in depth rasped across this land, erasing part of the geologic record and deeply furrowing what was left. Some of the world's oldest rock, up to 2.7 billion years old, has been exposed within the park.

Voyageurs was named for the French-Canadian canoeists who transported beaver and other pelts between Montreal and the Canadian Northwest by birchbark canoe in the late eighteenth and early nineteenth centuries. Today, roads lead only to the edges of the park, and canoes and other boats are the chief form of travel. In winter, cross-country skiing and snowmobiling are options. The howl of the wolf and the cry of the loon on a moonlit night are worth whatever trouble it took to reach this remote land of forest and water.

Mammoth Cave, in Kentucky, contains more than 330 miles of passageway explored and mapped

so far, making this by far the longest known cave system in the world. According to legend, the entrance to Mammoth Cave was discovered in 1797 by a hunter who was chasing a bear, or vice versa. The cave soon became a tourist attraction, one of the first in the United States. Stephen Bishop, a self-educated slave who was an early guide, gained a measure of fame beginning in the 1830s as he discovered more than twenty miles of passageway.

The cave has been dissolved out of limestone beds deposited more than 300 million years ago. Uplift of the land cracked the limestone, and water, working its way toward the nearby Green River, percolated through the cracks and gradually widened them. This sculpturing has produced immense interior spaces, including the 192-foot-high Mammoth Dome and the 105-foot-deep Bottomless Pit. Rivers flow far underground. Sparkling white gypsum crystals, stalactites, and stalagmites are among the embellishments.

In a world of perpetual darkness, eyes are useless, and many blind creatures have evolved, including fish, spiders, daddy longlegs, and beetles. The cave critters survive in part on dung dropped in the cave by bats and crickets paying visits from the world of light.

Wild ponies are a popular attraction on Assateague Island National Seashore, in Maryland and Virginia. Rounded up each July, they swim across a narrow inlet, and some foals are sold at auction, with proceeds supporting the local fire company.

PLAINS AND MOUNTAINS

Almost imperceptibly, the Great Plains slope downward from the base of the Rocky Mountains, falling from an altitude of six thousand feet in Colorado and Wyoming to about one thousand feet on merging with the Mississippi Valley. Across the four hundred miles from west to east, the decline is barely ten feet per mile. Buffalo no longer roam free by the millions nibbling native grasses, which have yielded to corn and wheat. Winds still blow and tumbleweeds still tumble, though now the terrain is laced with many fences. The Dust Bowl of the 1930s remains a warning to those who seek to cultivate the land without regard to the rules of nature.

Theodore Roosevelt, looking very much the innocent eastern dude, first traveled from his home in New York to the plains in the Dakota Territory in 1883. The bespectacled Harvard graduate took an unlikely interest in running a cattle ranch. After being devastated by the deaths of his wife and mother on the same day in 1884, Roosevelt returned to Dakota, to the town of Medora, and bought into one ranch and started building another. Soon he was running 4,500 head of cattle. The future president also hoped to hunt buffalo, but the wild herds had been virtually wiped out. "TR" was dismayed by the uncontrolled overgrazing that had destroyed the grasslands and reduced habitat for songbirds and small

Theodore Roosevelt, an eastern dude from New York City, fell in love with the wide open spaces of North Dakota, and he established a cattle ranch in this area. The badlands along the Little Missouri River are now included in Theodore Roosevelt National Park.

mammals. He eventually channeled most of his energies elsewhere, and sold out in 1898 before dashing off to Cuba to lead his Rough Riders in the Spanish-American War.

Roosevelt left the cattle country as a conservationist who later wrote, "I never would have been President if it had not been for my experiences in North Dakota." As president, Roosevelt established the U.S. Forest Service, signed the Antiquities Act, created eighteen national monuments, and approved five national parks and fifty-one wildlife refuges.

Roosevelt's ranch and surrounding badlands of the Little Missouri River are now preserved at Theodore Roosevelt National Park in southwestern North Dakota. Buffalo and elk have been reintroduced, and the sight of wild horses and Texas longhorns recall the ranching days of a century ago. Prairie dogs peer from their holes, watching for trouble and barking alarms. The meadowlark, "one of our sweetest, loudest songsters," according to Roosevelt, still perches atop a bush where "the Plains air seems to give it a voice." Here, needle and thread grass still bends to the unchallenged wind, and in summer titanic cumulonimbus clouds still pile up out of nowhere and deposit drenching but welcome rains. The park is a fitting tribute to our first conservation-minded president.

A cannonball concretion, fluted slopes, vertical joints, and caprock create a geological mosaic in the strangely eroded badlands of Theodore Roosevelt National Park.

A similar but much larger fragment of the Great Plains has been set aside in Badlands National Park in southwestern South Dakota. Early French-Canadian trappers called the region "bad lands to travel across," but visitors today, provisioned with water, need have no fear of venturing forth afoot or on wheels. Many geological forces, including outwash from highlands to the west and volcanic ash showers, helped create the bizarre shapes of the modern badlands. Although rain is scarce, the force of a few annual thunderstorms tears at the soft strata and shapes the land into a succession of pastel canyons, ridges, chimneys, pillars, toadstools, and other forms.

Weathering has also unmasked fossil evidence of an Oligocene menagerie, almost fascinating enough to make us wish we had lived thirty million years ago. We would have wandered among giant pigs, fierce saber-toothed cats, horses only twenty inches tall, rhinoceros ancestors twelve feet tall, and hideous sheeplike creatures sporting three pairs of horns on their faces.

The park lies within the one-time domain of the Dakota, or Sioux, nation, who ruled it aggressively after obtaining horses in the 1700s. The Sioux, in turn, fell before the advancing European-Americans. In 1890, at Stronghold Table within the present park, the Sioux took part in the Ghost Dance ceremony, which promised that the whites would depart and the buffalo would return. Mounting tensions led to tragedy. On December 29, 1890, at Wounded Knee, just south of the park, 153 Sioux and 25 soldiers were killed in the last armed conflict involving Native Americans and the U.S. Army. The Sioux now participate in the administration of the park.

Long, long ago, volcanoes to the west or southwest of present-day South Dakota released immense volumes of ash, which settled here and became the whitish layer near the top of the Badlands formation.

Early French-Canadian trappers, passing through what is now Badlands National Park, called the region les mauvaises terres a traverser ("bad lands to travel across"). Today, carrying sufficient water, hikers can explore the area in safety.

Flowstone and calcite crystals are among the lovely features of Jewel Cave National Monument in South Dakota. A pioneering husband-and-wife team led more than seven hundred trips into the cave, which is still being explored.

In Wind Cave National Park, in South Dakota, hidden beneath the serene grasslands carpeted with globemallows, lies an immense limestone cavern containing complex but delicate formations.

Today pronghorns, bison, and bighorn sheep roam the land, in far reduced (from the last century) but still welcome numbers. Golden eagles, turkey vultures, and marsh hawks circle the topless sky, watching for prairie dogs and other rodents. Badgers, coyotes, and prairie rattlesnakes join the modern menagerie.

West of the Badlands, in the Black Hills and at the eastern edge of that range are, respectively, Jewel Cave National Monument and Wind Cave National Park. These limestone caverns are among the loveliest anywhere, and with seventy-three miles of passageway, Jewel Cave is the world's fourth longest. The same upheaval that formed the Black Hills about sixty million years ago cracked the limestone and allowed flowing water to create these awesome subterranean natural art museums.

Jewel Cave is named for its most dramatic feature, the calcite crystals that sparkle like gems when illuminated. Stalactites and stalagmites have formed and often, as a result of the endless drip of mineral-laden water, one has joined the other to form columns. Water trickling down slanted ceilings has formed translucent draperies, and water spilling over a wall has left deposits of flowstone.

Nearby, one day in 1881, a hunter paused by a hole in the ground and was astonished when a strong wind from the hole blew off his hat. Thus Wind Cave was discovered and got its name. Shifts in atmospheric pressure inside and outside the cave cause the wind to blow first one way, then another. Wind Cave is renowned for its boxwork—the honeycomb-shaped calcite structures that protrude from walls and ceilings—the world's best example of this formation. Other formations include

In Badlands National Park in South Dakota, sediments laid down from 23 million to 37 million years ago have now been exposed by the erosive power of rain, wind, and frost. Spires, knobs, sharp ridges, and deep canyons are common features of the landscape.

Devils Tower, in Wyoming, resembles a giant tree stump. The 865-foot-deep shaft began as a mass of molten magma that formed underground. It then cooled, fractured into hexagonal columns, and was exposed by erosion.

Lower Falls and the Grand Canyon of the Yellowstone River in Yellowstone National Park. The canyon cuts through volcanic material that filled a vast caldera after an eruption. Hydrothermal activity bleached the dark rhyolite to create the pale yellow, orange, and white rock we see today.

"popcorn," a knobby growth resembling coral, and frostwork, crystals of calcite and argonite that resemble snowballs.

The Rocky Mountains, backbone of the continent, extend some 3,200 miles from western Alaska to Santa Fe, New Mexico, and are the most striking physiological feature of the United States and Canada. At the crest of the sequence of ranges, along the invisible line of the Continental Divide, raindrops falling inches apart flow, respectively, toward the Atlantic and Pacific oceans.

Young men who followed Horace Greeley's advice to go west found young mountains composed of very old rock thrown upward and fractured by powerful forces within the earth just sixty million years ago. And the new arrivals who took up prospecting found many treasures buried in the Rockies, including gold, silver, copper, salt, coal, lead, iron, gypsum, petroleum, and oil shale.

The mountains offered superior visual resources as well, including sharp peaks and rakishly tilted sedimentary formations. Scenes of moisture-filled clouds piling up atop the snow-covered Rockies would have been enough to inspire invention of the picture

Old Faithful, in Yellowstone, erupts, on average, every sixty-five to seventy-five minutes. An upwelling of magma, within two miles of the surface of the ground, heats the earth and the water then explodes upward into geysers.

Steam rises in winter from Firehole River in Yellowstone. The river is fed by hot water from geysers, but the fishing is excellent.

postcard. The variety and beauty of mountain flora is a dream come true for botanists and photographers. Wild animal herds flourished throughout the high country until most were reduced or wiped out by human predation. It is not surprising that the national park idea was born in the Rockies, in Yellowstone, and it has been advanced through the preservation of other choice mountain landscapes.

Yellowstone has never lost its preeminent position in the hearts and minds of Americans. This is true even though other units in the National Park System are larger and still others are more frequently visited. Yosemite Valley, in its design and detail, has, arguably, a special unsurpassed kind of beauty and grace. A number of parks are wilder than Yellowstone, or more equable in climate.

Yellowstone has many superlatives—ten thousand thermal features, for example—but the park cannot be appreciated through these numbers any more than one could understand the importance of Babe Ruth by reciting his stats. Born of legend, its very reality defended only by trappers and prospectors, the least credible of witnesses (at least as judged by eastern sophisticates), Yellowstone defied probability and emerged from its myths and the mists of its geysers. It emerged finally in its totality as a grand assemblage, an orchestra of plateau and canyon gorges, lakes, and high country, tempestuous in its steamy eruptions yet possessing an ultimate serenity concomitant with its great scale and mountain backdrop. The largest herds south of Alaska—twenty thousand elk, two thousand buffalo, plus hundreds of bears, deer, sheep, moose, and pronghorns—are the performers on this great stage.

On Mammoth Terrace, in Yellowstone, hot water deposits travertine (calcium carbonate), a form of limestone. New travertine is deposited every day in an ever-changing art show.

Yellowstone became the world's first national park. A member of an early expedition, sitting by a campfire, concluded that such a spectacular location should be preserved for all American citizens. Today, more than one hundred nations have established national parks.

Americans, millions of whom may never participate in a Loop Road autojam, feel possessive toward Yellowstone, and were incredulous in 1988 when fires burned out of control for months and reportedly "destroyed" much of the park. How could it have been allowed to happen there? The fires, which are an essential part of renewal in nature, did threaten property and park resources and constituted too much of a good thing, but the land rebounded, as opportunistic plants rose from the ashes to be nibbled upon by appreciative wildlife. Americans might redirect their concern to threats involving the grizzly population and the prospective tapping of geothermal energy outside the park that could shut off the eruptions inside the park. Yellowstone's 2.2 million acres are not enough to suit roaming animals, and if the park's resources are to survive, protection must be extended to adjacent national forests now subjected to mining and logging. The park is not yet secure and its future is uncertain.

About those "thermal features." Geyser function is not fully understood, so we can indulge our imaginations a bit. Suffice it to say that the earth's crust is unusually thin under the park, and indeed molten rock churns just two miles beneath the surface. Magma heats the earth, and water flowing through underground cracks then becomes heated, hence lighter, and rises in the vertical tubes of the

Winter is a difficult season for Yellowstone's population of twenty thousand elk. Food is hard to find, and some elk are killed by hunters when they wander outside the park in search of sustenance.

Bison (buffalo) graze in Hayden Valley in Yellowstone
National Park. The valley was named for Ferdinand Hayden,
who led the federal survey of the region in 1871. His expedition
established that rumors of a unique and beautiful land were true.

Morning Glory Pool lies in the Upper Geyser Basin in Yellowstone.
The park contains about ten thousand thermal features.

The Yellowstone country in northwestern Wyoming represents the American
West at its picture-perfect best. Water, cold and free, spills across green
meadows beneath robust mountains capped by clouds. Birdsong, gentle
breezes, and floral fragrances round out the sensory symphony.

The Tetons and Jackson Hole are part of the twelve-million-acre Greater Yellowstone eco-system. More of this acreage must be given stronger federal protection in order to safeguard animals that wander outside the parks and are shot.

The Teton Range in Wyoming is the boldest façade to confront anyone traveling westward toward the Rocky Mountains. Millions of years ago, a giant mass of rock split, north to south. The eastern half has slipped beneath the earth's surface, leaving these jagged peaks sharply outlined against the sky.

geysers. The water flashes into steam, which expands into the open-air displays that are unrivaled elsewhere in the world. Each geyser is unique, perhaps erupting hourly, perhaps yearly, some predictably, some without any apparent master plan.

Grand Teton National Park, a short drive to the south over John D. Rockefeller, Jr., Memorial Highway, is associated with Yellowstone in most people's minds, and in fact both are part of the Greater Yellowstone Ecosystem, the largest essentially intact natural area in the earth's temperate zones. Some large mammals migrate seasonally between the parks.

The rocks of the Grand Tetons are ancient, but the mountains themselves are as dynamic and youthful (geologically speaking) as they appear to be. Just nine million years ago, last year's calendar to earth scientists, the ancient rock split into two fault blocks. The faces of the two blocks began to slide against each other, the one to the west rising, the one to the east slipping. For this reason, the eastern face of the Tetons today is stark and abrupt, visible to its base, unobstructed by foothills. A sandstone strip atop Mount Moran, six thousand feet above the valley floor, once matched up with a layer of sediment now 25,000 feet below the surface of Jackson Hole to the east. Not that you'd notice it, but the Teton Range is still rising, at the rate of a foot every three or four centuries.

Glaciers pushed through in the much more recent past, but the mountaintops remained unscathed. The broad U-shaped valleys within the mountains and the glacial moraines at their feet evoke the power of the ice sheets.

Topographical features of Jackson Hole include Jackson Lake and many smaller lakes, the meandering Snake River, and buttes that rise from the valley. Wildflowers, often in carpets, spread across the valley in season, and conifers cling to the steep sides of the mountains.

Bald eagles and ospreys fish and nest along the river. Spring brings great blue herons to their rookery at Oxbow Bend. Migratory waterfowl rely on the ponds formed by the constructions of beavers. Nearly three thousand elk spend the summer in the park, then move south to the National Elk Refuge after snow begins to fall. Bison meander through the sagebrush country south of Jackson Lake, and moose work the rivers and streams, consuming aquatic plants. Mule deer and coyotes are prominent, but the bighorn sheep stay out of sight high on the mountains.

Rocky Mountain National Park, which encompasses a portion of the Front (eastern) Range of the Rockies in Colorado, provides a unique opportunity: easy access for most visitors to the lonely world of alpine tundra. The means of access for most visitors is Trail Ridge Road, a fifty-mile-long scenic

The Snake River, flowing east and then south from Jackson Lake in Grand Teton National Park, meanders through Jackson Hole as its waters begin a long journey toward the Pacific Ocean.

Jackson Lake occupies the northern portion of Jackson Hole, the broad valley at the base of the mountains in Grand Teton National Park. Aspen, which grow in dense groves, seem to set the landscape on fire when their leaves turn in autumn.

Bear Lake, accessible by road, is one of the most popular destinations in Rocky Mountain National Park. Trail Ridge Road, the park's principal auto route, climbs to 12,183 feet, and is covered by snow much of the year.

Rocky Mountain National Park, in Colorado, contains the largest concentration of fourteen-thousand-foot peaks in the United States outside Alaska. One-third of the park is above the treeline.

route that tops out at 12,183 feet, well above the tree line. The highest point in the park is the crest of Longs Peak, with an altitude of 14,255 feet.

The word "fragile," sometimes overused in describing various kinds of landscapes, seems altogether apt for the wind-whipped tundra of stunted plants and bare rock. The wind is so strong that the dried-out terrain is in effect a desert. The temporary absence of a snow cover allows a growing season that can be less than ten weeks long. Lichens and mosses cling to the exposed rock.

Mammalian life is surprisingly vigorous. Two herds of bighorns, symbols of the park, but now reduced to only two hundred individuals, roam the high country. Pocket gophers perform the good deed of churning the soil. Pikas store dried grasses in sheltered dens. Weasels and marmots scurry about. Among birds, only the ptarmigan spends the entire year above the tree line.

Waterton/Glacier International Peace Park sprawls across the international boundary between Alberta and Montana. Glacier National Park, on the American side, and its Canadian counterpart, Waterton, share similar high-mountain scenery, long and thin glacier-carved lakes, and abundant flora and fauna.

The region contains primarily sedimentary rock: mudstone, sandstone, and limestone. Long after deposition, Precambrian rock to the west, a billion years old, was pushed up, and it slid forty miles to the northeast until it rode over younger rock, creating an overthrust, an awesome rearranging of

Only a few thousand years ago, in what is now Craters of the Moon National Monument in Idaho, lava spewed out of the earth, and it has created a grotesque landscape of lava flows, caves, tubes, and spatter cones.

The dunes in Great Sand Dunes National Monument in Colorado are among the largest and highest in the United States. They were deposited over thousands of years by winds blowing through the passes of the Sangre de Cristo range, in the background.

Going-to-the-Sun Road passes Saint Mary Lake in
Glacier National Park. Two hundred lakes and hundreds
of waterfalls are among the natural features in the park.

Only fifty small glaciers remain in Glacier National Park in Montana, but the force of the former ice sheets is shown in the deeply gouged U-shaped valleys and sharp ridges that survived the assault of the ice.

geological strata. Today, the overthrust rock has become the Lewis Range, easternmost in the park, and it rises dramatically above the adjacent prairie.

Erosion worked on this design, and ice invaded the future park four times, scooping out valleys and pushing debris before it that now stands as hilly glacial moraines. Some fifty glaciers remain from the ice sheets, occupying amphitheaters, or cirques, high on the mountainsides.

Two hundred lakes and hundreds of waterfalls are additional gifts of the ice age. Virgin forests scale the mountains, and in autumn, the yellow mass of quaking aspen lights up the landscape. In the autumn, some 350 migrating golden and bald eagles fly down to McDonald Creek to feast on Kokanee salmon. Glacier is another of the few remaining redoubts of the grizzly and bighorn. Mountain goats, sporting long, shaggy white coats and upturned black horns, are at home on the steep slopes. The Going-to-the-Sun Road is the scenic rival to Rocky Mountain's Trail Ridge Road, though it ascends only to 6,664 feet at Logan Pass.

Rocky Mountain goats, who tend to be friendly and curious, are agile climbers who populate the steepest ledges and cliffs in the high altitudes of Glacier National Park.

CANYONS AND DESERTS

A desert, by strict definition, is an area receiving no more than ten inches of precipitation per year. Not all of the American Southwest thus qualifies as desert, and indeed green oases freshen the landscape. But the overall perception is one of dryness, of burning sun and naked rock and empty arroyos, of wind that sings as it churns up stinging grains of sand, of cracked earth and lined faces, of lizards scurrying for shade and furtive mammals—hunters and hunted—who venture forth only in the cool of the night.

To those who linger in the desert long enough to fall in love with it, a far more complex and subtle picture emerges. Plants and animals in surprising variety have all developed strategies for surviving in the harsh climate. The rocks themselves tell a story of hundreds of millions of years of geological change that can be read with pleasure by observant explorers.

And finally it is water itself, in scarce supply but by no means absent, that ultimately shapes and designs the arid land and provides its most dramatic moments. The joke about the so-called two-inch rain—the raindrops fall two inches apart—reflects the frustration of cattlemen and dirt farmers who need an occasional break from the sunlight. But rain really does come, often all at once. One can often stand at the edge of the Grand Canyon or at some other vantage point and see three or more thunderstorms in progress.

Rain can be gentle, but it is more often drenching, and as the rainwater spills across the hard earth and pours into dry streambeds, flash floods occur. The roiling mass of opaque water, snagging outcrops of dirt and small trees and other debris as it surges forward, eventually

Flowing westward out of the Rocky Mountains, the Colorado River begins its great task of shaping and sculpturing the red-rock country of the American Southwest. The cliffs of Colorado National Monument, in the western part of the state, rise above Grand Valley.

The surreal landscape of Dinosaur National Monument, in Colorado and Utah, seems even spookier when one remembers that this area was once the home of stegosaurus and brontosaurus, whose bones may be seen here.

About 145 million years ago, dinosaurs became common in this part of Colorado and Utah. When some of the beasts died, floodwaters washed their carcasses onto a sandbar, where other sediments buried the remains. Erosion stripped off the younger rocks, and paleontologists are excavating the bones.

The steep and deep gray walls of the Black Canyon of the Gunnison are shrouded in shadow most of the time, hence the name of this national monument in Colorado. Swallows, eagles, hawks, and vultures live on the cliffs, and soar on updrafts.

In Arches National Park, iron in trace amounts in the entrada sandstone produces the bright orange coloration. The entrada has eroded into bizarre shapes throughout the canyon country of southern and eastern Utah.

enters larger creeks and pushes onto one of the desert's major rivers. The Colorado and the Rio Grande are the master streams. These drainages, including their myriad tributaries, have sculptured the land, producing the distinct shapes of buttes, mesas, and canyons. The Colorado system, in particular, has created myriad curious rock forms.

To trace the Colorado from its source is to take a trip through two billion years of geological time. Such a journey also takes the traveler along a nearly unbroken chain of starkly beautiful parklands. "The River of the Shining Mountains" rises in the Never Summer Range near the Continental Divide in central Colorado, and works its way southwest, picking up side stream flows in a fairly conventional manner until it breaks out of the Rockies and rips into the sedimentary strata of the Colorado Plateau. Colorado National Monument, near the Utah border, is just a twenty-thousand-acre sandstone tease, its walls and monoliths a bare hint of what is to come.

The serious scenery begins inside Utah as the river deepens its channel and forms most of the southern border of Arches National Park. The Great Sculptor took his (or her) time in creating the two hundred or so openings in the rock that the park contains today—the world's largest collection of stone arches. The story begins 300 million years ago when an ocean basin formed

and salt deposits accumulated at the bottom of the basin. Massive deposits of sand and sediments spread atop the three thousand feet of salt and hardened into stone. The weight pushed the salt down in places, but the salt was forced up elsewhere if the rock cover was thinner. The upward pressure and subsequent regional uplift cracked the rock in a sequence of long parallel lines called joints. The rock resembles sliced bread, but with the slices still together as in a loaf. Gradually water and ice and the roots of plants worked into the joints and began to leverage the slices apart. They became freestanding fins. Then more weathering typically occurred at the base of the fins and pieces of the rock fell away to produce holes. Gravity and further weathering opened the holes to create arches.

Landscape Arch, at 291 feet, is so thin that it might snap in two at any time—maybe even in the next million years.

The prize among arches requires some effort, a fairly steep ascent up a slickrock slope through a multicolored rock jungle, then a careful walk along a narrow ledge on a sheer cliff, and then it appears: Delicate Arch, a staple of landscape calendars, perfect in its shape and scale, poised on the lip of a deep sandstone bowl, framing the distant—sometimes snow-covered—La Sal Mountains,

At 291 feet in length, Landscape Arch is just nine feet shorter than a football field. Arches form when weaker underlying rock is removed by weathering or breaks off in chunks, creating and then enlarging openings.

Turret Arch in Arches National Park. About
two hundred arches have been catalogued
in the park. Some are remote and difficult
to find, and arch "collectors" pursue them
as if they were birders compiling a life list.

Delicate Arch in Arches National Park,
perched on the lip of a deep sandstone
bowl, is an inspiration to hikers who
make the effort to reach it by way of
a steep climb and a narrow ledge. The
La Sal Mountains provide a backdrop.

glowing orange in the late afternoon sun. Hikers sit mesmerized, stunned, out of breath in its presence. No photograph can do it justice because Delicate Arch can be appreciated fully only within the totality of its setting—the stone wilderness rolling away in every direction—primeval, uncompromising, endless for all one can tell, uncivilized majesty.

Arches National Park lies northeast of the town of Moab, the obvious base for exploring the wild country of eastern Utah. The scenery, it should be noted, doesn't stop at the boundaries of the parks. The Colorado River swings past Moab and, after more goosenecking, enters Canyonlands National Park. This park is a canyon-country Louvre, a museum preserving much of what makes the Southwest special. Here one can find some of the world's most important examples of primitive rock paintings, some of the most dramatic deep canyon scenery, and surely the world's most extravagant collection of geological sculpture.

The Green and Colorado rivers unite within the park, and the Confluence Overlook becomes a mecca for surefooted hikers who look down into the shadows and try to understand how the two rivers could have wrought such erosional destruction. South of the confluence, the Colorado enters Cataract Canyon, where it drops eight feet per mile, a steeper rate than in the Grand Canyon.

The very earliest and latest sunlight produces the most vivid colors on the red rocks of the Southwest. This formation near the campground in Arches was photographed just before sunset.

Rainbow Bridge, in southern Utah, the world's largest natural bridge, soars to a height of 290 feet. Led by Paiute guides into a remote and labyrinthine wasteland of rock, white men saw the bridge for the first time in 1909.

Thrill-seekers in rubber rafts floating through the Big Drop descend thirty feet in one mile, a degree of slope offering an experience that may seem comparable to falling down a flight of stairs.

Canyonlands has few miles of paved roads, and the dirt roads are so pernicious you might rather walk. The park is a wilderness without the saving grace of handsome green forests. It is a paradox—so formidable to approach that it becomes a challenge to be met, so grotesque in design that it becomes compellingly beautiful.

River rafters, hardly recovered from the trauma of the Big Drop, soon encounter an unsettling calm. The forward movement of the raft ceases and the froth of the whitewater fades. The voyagers have exited the park and entered Glen Canyon National Recreation Area, which is synonymous with Lake Powell. The motor is turned on and the raft proceeds to the takeout landing. Lake Powell is almost two hundred miles long.

A trip southwest on the lake brings one past tributaries of the buried river that lead to other natural shrines. Natural Bridges National Monument, to the south, contains three huge stone bridges. These may resemble arches but they are created by the flow of water in a streambed. During flash floods, rushing water moving through a loop in a stream course slams into a tall fin of rock and

The Colorado River, early morning, Canyonlands National Park. Most of the plant and animal life flourishes along the rivers. Boats, preferably ones without motors, can bring visitors into the heart of the haunting beauty of the narrow gorges.

Several giant rock "stairsteps" lead down from the Colorado Plateau to the Green and Colorado rivers, which meet in the heart of Canyonlands National Park in Utah. The highest and tallest stratum, the Wingate sandstone, splits off in thin slabs that shatter on the ground below.

eventually punches a hole in the rock. The water then takes a short cut, rushing through the hole and enlarging it. Weathering further widens the opening, and a natural bridge is the result.

The Dirty Devil River enters Lake Powell from the north, and one of its tributaries, the Fremont River, courses through the Waterpocket Fold, the principal geological feature of Capitol Reef National Park.

The Fold, about one hundred miles long and nearly straight as an arrow for most of its length, was created sixty million years ago when earth forces pushed up sedimentary rock and left it pointed upward to the west at about a 45° angle. Time then eroded a portion of the rock, and what is left thrusts boldly out of the ground as one of the most spectacular landforms in the United States. The western façade of the fold is a geological textbook written in stone.

At the base of the fold are the chocolate-colored sandstones, siltstones, and mudstones of the Moenkopi Formation. Ripple marks left in the sand by the lapping waters at a shoreline are still dramatically visible 200 million years later. Amphibians swimming in the shallow water slapped the sand with their fins and these fin marks are visible today.

The Moenkopi is topped in places by the Shinarump Conglomerate. Its sometimes hummocky

The Green River is visible in the distance below this overlook in Canyonlands National Park. Few people had seen this vast and empty region before the 1950s, when a uranium boom sent prospectors stampeding into the canyon country.

Capitol Reef National Park in Utah has been called the Land of the Sleeping Rainbow because of the striped rock of many colors that reaches from horizon to horizon. Each stratum is a fascinating chapter in the earth's geological history.

Imaginations can run wild in Bryce Canyon. This photograph seems to suggest a game of three-dimensional chess, with rooks and bishops occupying all of the squares.

Bryce Canyon National Park, in Utah, is not a canyon at all, but rather an amphitheater, which faces out onto a broad valley. As the plateau erodes backward, more of these colorful spires will emerge.

Thor's Hammer on the Navajo Loop Trail in Bryce Canyon National Park. Trails, which begin at the rim, are very steep, and the climb back up the amphitheater will be slow going.

appearance gave rise to its irreverent name: Shinar is the Paiute word for wolf, and rump is an English slang word needing no elaboration. The Shinarump, representing the deposits of streambeds, is a source of uranium that is found in its petrified wood. The Shinarump is the bottom layer of the Chinle Formation, which comes from various watery environments and volcanic ash. The Chinle forms gentle soft mounds in pastels of green, gray, pink, blue, and purple.

The massive sheer cliffs of Wingate sandstone rise hundreds of feet above the Chinle and flare brightly in the late sunlight. As the soft underlying Chinle erodes away, the Wingate breaks off in giant blocks that scatter across the terrain. The Kayenta Formation, atop the Wingate, resembles it in color and shape. The Wingate-Kayenta cliffs are usually stained by dark stripes of desert varnish, which may be formed when water carrying concentrations of manganese and iron spills down the face of the cliff. The ancients scratched petroglyphs into the varnished surfaces, using the lighter rock beneath to achieve a pleasing artistic effect.

The Navajo Sandstone domes top off the Waterpocket Fold. The Navajo was delivered to the canyon country 175 million years ago by winds that blew first one way and then another. These shifts in direction are still evident in the many-angled cross-bedding in this sandstone. The Navajo domes resemble the domes of capitol buildings, giving Capitol Reef part of its name. "Reef" is a reference to the Fold itself.

Rainbow Bridge, the world's largest and undoubtedly most beautiful natural bridge, spans a side canyon off Lake Powell, and is easily accessible by boat. *Nonnezoshi*, Navajo for "rainbow of stone," arches upward 290 feet, and the U.S. Capitol building could be placed beneath it.

Below Glen Canyon Dam, just across the border in Arizona, the Paria River enters from the north. The Paria heads at the base of the amphitheater beneath the thousands of slender, graceful formations in a panoply of colors that constitute Bryce Canyon National Park.

Bryce Canyon is better seen than written about, because language has no words to describe adequately its spectacle, the sheer mass of its pinnacles and spires and the delicacy of its colors. The formations one sees today were laid down as silt at the bottom of a lake. The soft siltstone has eroded readily under pressure of falling rain and of ice expanding between cracks in the rock. Iron (adding reds) and manganese (adding blues and lavenders) have colored the rock.

The Paiute name for Bryce translates as "Red rocks standing like men in a bowl-shaped canyon." That's rather straightforward, and no wordsmith can improve upon it.

Large lakes once occupied the Bryce Canyon area, and sediments deposited at the bottom of the lakes are now eroding into these formations. Iron and manganese contribute colors, and the rocks seem illuminated from within.

The Towers of the Virgin, Zion National Park, Utah. The walls in this part of Zion Canyon are cut through the Navajo Sandstone. It was laid down as sand dunes in the Jurassic era, which also produced the dinosaurs.

Unlike the Grand Canyon, which visitors usually approach at the rim, Zion Canyon is accessible by a road that follows the Virgin River, and visitors can appreciate the height and power of the rock walls that tower above them.

The shifting winds of Jurassic times can be seen in the cross-bedding in the Navajo Sandstone formations in Zion. The quartz crystals were carried here from distant mountains, and now erosion is wearing them loose again.

Zion, the westernmost of Utah's five national parks, has been shaped largely by the Virgin River, another tributary of the Colorado. The speed with which running water sculptures the land depends on what kind of rock it must contend with. The dominant rock layer at Zion is the Navajo Sandstone, which at Capitol Reef forms the domes above the Waterpocket Fold. In Zion, the Navajo is nearly one-half mile in thickness. The Great White Throne and other formations in Zion Canyon are carved in this sandstone. Throughout the canyon, water working its way through the porous sandstone spills and trickles down the cliffs, and hanging gardens of columbine, monkeyflower, and other plants decorate the rock walls.

Further up Zion Canyon, the river is forced to cut through the much more resistant Kayenta Formation. Here the canyon narrows to twenty feet in width, and it is two thousand feet in depth. These narrows, some sixteen miles in length, provide one of the spookiest, most memorable hikes in the Southwest.

In some places in Zion, the canyon walls are so close that hikers can place both hands on opposite sides at the same time. Tragically, lives have been lost when flash floods upstream sent sheets of water through these slots in the rock.

One must wade through the stream channel, which is often filled with water wall to wall. The half-mile climb from the canyon floor and the hiking available in Zion's vast backcountry amply reward the energetic explorer.

The Grand Canyon, nature's most ambitious excavation project, extends for 277 miles through the plateau of northern Arizona. Many millions of people from around the world have stood at the rims and stared at the canyon, and a far smaller number have walked down into the gorge or floated through it. Occasionally a tourist can be heard to exclaim, "There's a river down there!" Many visitors have only the faintest idea of what they're looking at or how it got that way. They choose simply to savor the beauty of the canyon, as when the mesas and buttes rising within the gorge are touched by the early or late sun or when they are skiffed with snow.

But any understanding of the abyss, let alone a heightened appreciation of its beauty, requires one to consider the canyon as a chronicle of life on earth. At the rim you can observe sea shells deposited in the limestone a mere 250 million years ago. But at the bottom, a vertical mile below the South Rim, you can touch granite two billion years old, appropriately black, and devoid of fossils because it was created in a world that knew no life in any form. When walking out of the canyon on foot, remember that each step up the trail represents a thousand years of earth history. Hikers must climb up past the remains of the crablike trilobites, past the age of fishes, and through a limestone graveyard containing the crushed remains of myriad oysterlike creatures. They then walk among the footprints of short-legged amphibians, past delicate fossil tracings of primitive ferns in which a few insect-wings commingle, and up the frozen dunes of the Coconino sandstone.

The climb brings hikers to three life zones otherwise widely distributed across the face of the earth. These are the Lower Sonoran Zone with its agave, cactus, yucca, lizards, and rattlesnakes; the Upper Sonoran Zone, featuring the dwarf forest of pinyon and juniper; and the Transition Zone, with its ponderosa groves enlivened by the calls of the chickadee and the Steller's

The rocks in the Grand Canyon are very old—up to two billion years old at the bottom of the canyon, some of the oldest rocks exposed anywhere on the earth. And yet, the canyon itself is quite young, geologically speaking, having been excavated by the Colorado River in about seven million years.

Standing at the rim of the Grand Canyon in 1903, President Theodore Roosevelt declared that man could not improve on the canyon and that it must be preserved for future generations.

Clouds flow across the Grand Canyon, adding to the drama of the scene below. The interplay of light and cloud throughout the day and the seasons ensures that the canyon will always differ in appearance.

The view from Yavapai Point, on the South Rim of the Grand Canyon.

jay. Perhaps it is this double and concurrent passage, through geological time and biological space, in this extraordinary setting, that enables the explorer to transcend the customary limits of a three-dimensional world.

A different kind of passage through the canyon, by rubber raft or wooden dory, carries the courageous through one or two weeks of whitewater—the world's premier waterborne adventure. In quiet moments, perhaps after beaching at a sandy campsite, one can explore the unknown worlds of hanging waterfalls and bottomless swimming pools in undulating side canyons too narrow to receive the direct illumination of the sun.

Near the bottom of the Grand Canyon, the Havasupai, the "people of the blue-green water," live in the village of Supai, accessible only by a sixty-five-mile road and an eight-mile trip by horseback or afoot down a precipitous trail.

Exiting from the Grand Canyon, the Colorado River flows west into Lake Mead National

Recreation Area. The lake was created by the construction of Hoover Dam, one of the world's most remarkable engineering achievements, on the Arizona-Nevada border. Below the dam, the diminished river resumes its course south toward the Gulf of California. The states through which it passes withdraw huge quantities of its water for irrigation and power, reducing the river to barely a trickle as it crosses into Mexico. The demise of the Colorado, short of the open sea, is a sad end for the river that, with its tributaries, has given form to a dozen national parks and monuments.

Four national parks lie within the drainage of the Southwest's other master stream, the Rio Grande. Colorful badlands topography similar to that found in the Dakotas is protected in Petrified Forest National Park in northeastern Arizona. The park includes a portion of the

In the 1960s, leaders of the environmental movement narrowly prevented federal approval of the construction of a dam in the Grand Canyon. A dam would have ruined the canyon's natural appearance and ended the down-cutting of the river through the gorge, one of the most dramatic ongoing stories in geology.

The dunes at White Sands National Monument in New Mexico are eroded off of massive layers of gypsum rock in nearby mountains. Several species of mice, lizards, and insects have evolved a white coloration as a means of avoiding predators.

Sunset Crater Volcano National Monument, in northern Arizona. The eruption that occurred here nine hundred years ago drove the Native Americans away, but they returned when they discovered that the volcanic deposits in the area produced excellent soil for the growing of crops.

Painted Desert, with its rocks colored red, pink, purple, lavender, pale green, chocolate, and gray. Two hundred million years ago, many streams flowed through the area, which was populated by animals resembling alligators and hippopotamuses, not to mention dinosaurs. Fossils of the enduring, if not endearing, cockroach have also turned up.

The park was established to protect rather more fascinating fossils, those of conifers up to two hundred feet tall that toppled over and were washed by swollen streams into a floodplain. Silt, mud, and volcanic ash covered the trunks, cutting off oxygen and slowing the decay of the trees. Ground waters bearing silica seeped through the logs and replaced the original wood tissues with silica deposits. The silica hardened and the logs became petrified wood. Harder rock covered the area, and it in turn was eroded away. Now the soft strata containing the fossil logs have been exposed. The logs have broken into chunks in a variety of sizes and a riot of color.

Here, the erosion is swift, and each gullywasher brings with it the promise of new surprises. In 1984 a large dinosaur nicknamed Gertie turned up, and scientists are still trying to figure out whether this lizardlike animal was indeed a true reptile.

El Malpais National Monument, added to the Park System in 1987, is an eerie northwestern New Mexico landscape that shows the marks of volcanic violence. This seldom-seen wilderness contains cinder mountains, hollow lava tubes as large as subway passages, and caves filled with ice that never melts.

In southern New Mexico, White Sands National Monument showcases the world's largest gypsum dunefield, covering 230 square miles. The brilliant white dunes rise to sixty feet in height.

In Petrified Forest National Park, in Arizona, soft sedimentary layers like these erode quickly, by geological standards, and fossils of trees and of dinosaurs and other prehistoric animals continue to be discovered.

Farther south, the Guadalupe Mountains, which lie across the New Mexico-Texas border, are home to two national parks, one in each state. In New Mexico, the Carlsbad Caverns were formed within a great reef of rock. Rain water, acidified by air and soil, worked its way beneath the surface and dissolved underground limestone chambers. The creation of decorations within the cave, including draperies, flowstone, and cave pearls, has taken place in the last half-million years, all the result of water dripping into the cave. Each drop leaves a crystal of calcite, the building block of the decorations.

During spring, summer, and early fall, 300,000 Mexican free-tail bats live in the caves, sleeping by day attached to the ceiling. One square foot may contain up to three hundred bats. At dusk, they exit the caverns en masse to hunt for insects.

*The Rio Grande below Big Bend National Park
has been designated a wild and scenic river.*

*One of the newest additions to the park system is El Malpais (Spanish
for "the badlands") National Monument in New Mexico. Part of this
volcanic area was formed as recently as one thousand years ago. Ice
caves and a seventeen-mile lava tube are among the natural features.*

*This petrified wood is not wood at all. While the fallen trees were still
buried by silt, mud, and volcanic ash, silica-bearing groundwater seeped
through the logs and replaced the original wood tissue with silica
deposits. The silica hardened and the logs were later exposed by erosion.*

Great Basin National Park encompasses a representative sample of
Nevada's basin-and-range topography.
In addition to Wheeler Peak, shown
here, the park includes a forest of
bristlecone pines (foreground), which are
among the world's oldest living things.

In Big Bend National Park,
named for the U-shaped turn
taken by the river, the Rio Grande
forms the boundary between
Texas and Mexico. Santa Elena
Canyon is one of the scenic
highlights for river-runners.

The Guadalupe Mountains are part of an ancient marine fossil reef, one of the world's finest examples of the type. Incongruous as it seems today, as one stands in the desert, the reef was formed underwater, by sponges and other marine organisms that secreted lime. The sea evaporated, and the reef was buried under other sediments until the whole area was uplifted and the reef partly re-exposed. Guadalupe Mountains National Park incorporates the highlands, canyons, and portions of the surrounding desert. In The Bowl, a forested depression atop the mountains, elk, deer, mountain lions, and black bears roam. McKittrick Canyon is a verdant spring-fed oasis that has been called "the most beautiful spot in Texas."

Big Bend National Park is named for the lazy U-shape in the Rio Grande, which forms 107 miles of the park's southern boundary separating Texas and Mexico. The deep limestone canyons of the Rio Grande are popular with river-runners. But the park has two other "worlds," the Chihuahua Desert and the Chisos Mountains. Taken together, the three environments provide refuge for an unusually rich flora and fauna. Nearly four hundred species of birds are found here, more than in any other park. The roadrunner, preferring land to the air, hugs the ground, checking out the lizards and grasshoppers.

The underground passageways in Carlsbad Caverns National Park in New Mexico contain an unusually large array of formations, including stalagmites, stalactites, soda straws, draperies, flowstone, cave pearls, and popcorn.

After Carlsbad Caverns was carved out, rainwater seeped through the ground and absorbed limestone. Each drop deposited its tiny mineral load inside the cave as a crystal of calcite. Billions of such drops created these formations. The Giant Dome is sixty-two feet high.

In Saguaro National Monument, these cacti attain a height of fifty feet and have become the symbol of the Sonoran Desert of Arizona and Mexico. During its two-hundred-year life, a saguaro may produce forty million seeds, yet only one may grow into another cactus.

Organ Pipe Cactus National Monument in southern Arizona honors this immense cactus. Some specimens have sixty arms or more. Blossoms appear in the spring at the tip of each arm.

The massive buttress in the background, in Guadalupe Mountains National Park, was created underwater! When Texas was covered by a vast tropical ocean, marine organisms deposited lime to form a limestone reef, later exposed by upward pressures from within the earth and by erosion.

If winter rains have been sufficient, springtime in the desert features a carpet of wildflowers. The strange-looking "tree" in Joshua Tree National Monument, in California, is actually a yucca. Mormon pioneers thought the trees resembled Joshua raising his arms to the Lord.

Far from being "deserted," the Sonoran Desert in Organ Pipe Cactus National Monument is covered with many fascinating plants. These plants, as well as many animals and birds, survive summer temperatures that may reach 115°F.

Saguaro flowers bloom after dark and wilt by the following afternoon. But others take their place, and as many as one hundred flowers may appear on a single saguaro plant over a four-week period.

This headlike formation seems to be a brooding specter of death itself. Although early travelers were anxious to get through Death Valley, its reputation as a place where one might find death was greatly exaggerated.

Spring comes early to the desert, with wildflower displays in March. The Texas bluebonnet (lupine) is prominent, and the park also contains some sixty kinds of cacti. Snakes abound, including four kinds of rattlesnakes.

The Great Basin is the physiographical feature occupying the state of Nevada and portions of adjacent states. Low, narrow mountain ranges rise from the otherwise flat terrain. Created when blocks of the earth's crust became faulted on both sides and were uplifted, the ranges extend from north to south and have been likened to worms crawling from Canada to Mexico. Great Basin National Park, our forty-ninth park, was established in eastern Nevada in 1986 to preserve a portion of this environment.

The Snake Range, topped off by Wheeler Peak at 13,063 feet, dominates the park. Lehman Caves, on the flank of Wheeler Peak, contains huge fluted columns of various colors. The trail to the summit of the peak passes several alpine lakes and leads to an ancient bristlecone

California's Death Valley National Monument can fairly be described as the starkest, driest, hottest, and emptiest landscape in the United States. For those who love the unusual patterns and designs found in nature, the valley is also a source of endless fascination.

Wandering among the trees of the Giant Forest in Sequoia National Park and through sunlit meadows bordering the groves, one is humbled by the capacity of nature to create life. A tree 250 feet tall has grown from a seed so small that ninety thousand of them would weigh only one pound.

No roads traverse the high country of these two parks, and this kingdom is reserved for the strong-legged children of John Muir, the inheritors of its chill beauty, of its pale granite domes and turquoise lakes and runty flowers.

Yosemite is forty miles north of Kings Canyon. The appeal of its "incomparable valley" has been duly noted. Yosemite, too, has groves of sequoias up to 2,700 years old, and its high country has earned acclaim barely secondary to the valley. Glacier Point, a lookout accessible by automobile, provides the ultimate high country "high." At your feet, a sheer cliff drops 3,200 feet to the valley. Across the valley, Yosemite Falls, the world's second highest waterfall, plunges 2,425 feet in two straight drops broken by a series of cascades. To the right, Vernal and Nevada Falls transport the waters of the Merced River down stair steps to the valley. Beyond the valley the polished peaks of the High Sierra roll on as if waves of the sea.

The Tioga Pass Road leads across the top of Yosemite, past lakes, streams, and the ubiquitous granite. Tuolumne Meadows, the Sierra's largest high-mountain meadows, is a wildflower-dotted spread of natural beauty and an exploration base for hikers, backpackers, and crosscountry skiers.

Yosemite Falls (2,425 feet high) is one of many waterfalls that spill from the valley's rim to the Merced River. When glaciers scooped out the valley, water in streams flowing across the high country had nowhere to go but straight down.

The coast redwoods, once widely distributed in the northern latitudes, have been in retreat for some time. The glaciers overran much of their territory, leaving a relative remnant along 450 miles of the northern California coast. Loggers, as noted, further reduced their numbers, and the surviving redwoods today are found in a checkerboard of federal parklands and three state parks just below the Oregon border.

Cool summers, abetted by fog rolling off the sea, and mild wet winters combine to provide the great amount of moisture that the trees require. Other tall trees, including hemlock, fir, and spruce, also flourish within the parks. Altogether, more than one thousand kinds of plants and animals, including 350 species of birds, are found in Redwood National Park and the state parks. In a Brobdingnagian environment, even rhododendrons grow to thirty feet. The typical mature redwood may attain 200 to 250 feet in height over a lifetime of 400 to 800 years, but some individual trees live for 2,000 years, and the tallest tree has been measured at 367.8 feet. Most trails in the parks are short, but they provide a quick payoff, leading immediately into the damp, dark forest.

Many visitors never venture into the high country above Yosemite Valley. Those who do find sparkling lakes, like Tenaya, shown here, as well as plenty of wild-flowers and other plants that flourish during the short, mild summer.

Fog, cool summers, and mild winters provide the climate necessary to the growth of the coast redwoods in Redwood National Park and in several California state parks. The red-woods, the world's tallest living things, grow in cathedral-like groves that leave visitors pleasant-ly cut off from the outside world.

Sandy beaches with surf punctuated by sea stacks highlight thirty-five miles of coast. Majestic Roosevelt elk roam the shore and gray whales, porpoises, and seals can be sighted in the ocean.

Just thirty miles west of the teeming (with humanity) mainland of southern California, great colonies of sea mammals and sea birds flourish on Channel Islands National Park. The park is surrounded by the waters of the Channel Islands National Marine Sanctuary. The islands are an archaeological treasure, too, having been occupied by the Chumash Indians for thousands of years. Five of the eight islands are included in the park. They are accessible only by boat, and amenities are few.

Broad grasslands, high mountains with deeply cut canyons, and rolling hills are found on one or more of the islands. Steep cliffs rise from the sea. Beaches and other available nooks and

Muir Woods National Monument, a redwood forest north of San Francisco, was named in 1908 for the naturalist John Muir, who respond-ed: "This is the best tree lover's monument that could be found in all the forests of all the world."

Point Reyes National Seashore, on California's Pacific Coast. During the 1906 earthquake that devastated San Francisco, this peninsula moved almost twenty feet to the northwest.

crannies are occupied by wildlife. Fur-bearing mammals—otters, seals, and sea lions—have recovered from the days when they were hunted virtually to extinction. The three-ton northern elephant seals form breeding colonies. Steller sea lions, California sea lions, and northern fur seals are among other animals that gather together, barking, staking out territory, and all in all creating a general uproar.

The ocean is filled with creatures ranging from the blue whale, the world's largest animal, to microscopic plankton, the bottom link of the sea world's food chain. Sea birds, including gulls, cormorants, oystercatchers, and the endangered brown pelican, also nest here. Owls, kestrels, and larks fly over from the mainland. The island fox, no bigger than a cat, roams the uplands. Stands of giant coreopsis, or "tree sunflower," up to ten feet tall, thrive in summer.

Pinnacles National Monument, in central California, features the jagged remnants of a volcano. The notorious San Andreas Rift Zone, an instigator of volcanism, lies just east of the monument.

THE RING OF FIRE

Volcanic activity can be destructive of natural environments, and also of human life and property. But the upwelling of magma (molten rock) can also be a creative force, designing mountains that resemble pyramids and distributing ash and lava that are fascinating in their own right. The world's principal volcanic zone is found along and near the rims of the Pacific Ocean, at the edges of the tectonic plates that form the earth's crust. Volcanism is triggered as these great slabs override or grind past each other. As the expanding ocean crust pushes under the continental plates, it penetrates deeply enough into the earth to be partly remelted. Magma then erupts and creates volcanic mountains.

That, briefly, is the theory of plate tectonics. The reality is spectacular, all along the so-called Ring of Fire, which follows the rims of the ocean where the plates meet. Many of America's greatest natural monuments are volcanic mountains, and three volcanic national parks are found within the Pacific Ocean itself.

The National Park of American Samoa became the fiftieth park in 1988. The U.S.

One of the earth's most active volcanoes is Kilauea, on the "Big Island" of Hawaii in Hawaii Volcanoes National Park. Kilauea's crater is three miles across and several hundred feet deep.

The National Park of American Samoa was authorized in 1988. Some 2,300 miles south of Hawaii, these isolated volcanic islands are home to myriad wildlife, rain forests, coral reefs, and white sand beaches. In Samoan legend, these islets represent two lovers.

Trust Territory of American Samoa is 2,500 miles east of Australia in the South Pacific. American Samoa consists of five volcanic islands and two coral atolls, the only American soil south of the equator. The harbor and chief population center is at Pago Pago.

Volcanic activity under the ocean built up submarine mountains that eventually broke out above sea level. The largest island, Tutuila, consists of the eroded remnants of four volcanoes. Closely spaced streams have deeply eroded the mountains and left a mere skeletal backbone of mountain peaks and ridges running the length of the island. Other islands are the remnants of single volcanoes.

Days are warm and nights are balmy. Frequent rains have produced a tropical rainforest rich in flora and fauna. Two species of flying foxes, or fruit bats, may be seen by day, searching for fruit and flowers. Many birds nest along shores lined with steep cliffs inaccessible to humans. Marine life includes hawksbill turtles, who nest on the islands, and humpback whales. Snorkelers and scuba divers can explore extensive coral reefs.

Some 2,300 miles northeast of American Samoa, the classic chain of the Hawaiian Islands rises from the sea. Hawaii's two parks are Hawaii Volcanoes National Park on the "Big Island" of Hawaii and Haleakala National Park on Maui.

The elegant silversword rises in dramatic contrast to the moonscape volcanic surface of the earth in Haleakala National Park. The silversword is a member of the sunflower family. It may have gotten its start in Maui when seeds were carried by the wind from the Americas.

Mauna Loa and Kilauea are the active volcanoes on Hawaii. Mauna Loa and a nearby volcanic peak, Mauna Kea, both rise more than thirteen thousand feet above sea level. And, to offer a somewhat inapt metaphor, that is only the tip of the iceberg! The ocean floor lies some eighteen thousand feet below sea level, which means that Mauna Kea and Mauna Loa are both more than 31,000 feet in height and are in fact considered to be the greatest mountain masses on earth. (Mount Everest is 29,028 feet above sea level.) Mauna Loa started growing three million years ago, and required the first two million years just to get as high as sea level. It has erupted hundreds of thousands of times.

Kilauea is only some four thousand feet above sea level, but it has been extremely active (especially during the 1980s and early 1990s) and grows fast in geological terms. Kilauea's last truly violent eruption—accompanied by salvos of rocks, clouds of poison, and showers of hot mud—occurred in 1924. Its recent displays have been generally safe to view from a respectful distance and consist of tides of fiery red lava spilling down the slopes of the volcano. Several craters have formed on the slopes of Kilauea, and incandescent material pours from their vents. Both Kilauea and Mauna Loa have summit basins called calderas that are two to three miles across and several hundred feet deep.

Meanwhile, if you can wait, nature is building more seamounts on the ocean floor southeast of Hawaii. One is fifteen thousand feet high, or just three thousand feet below sea level. Humanoids of the far future will attend Rotary conventions there and loll on its sandy beaches.

One slope of the massive Haleakala Crater in Haleakala National Park on the Hawaiian island of Maui. Cinder cones and lava flows are prominent inside the crater, but no volcanic activity has occurred since 1790.

Molten lava flows into the sea after an eruption on one of the volcanoes on the island of Hawaii. The magma that spills from Kilauea and Mauna Loa is propelled upward from fifty miles beneath the surface of the earth.

Lassen Peak, in Lassen Volcanic National Park in California, has been dormant since 1921. The park encompasses a fascinating collection of jagged craters, steaming sulfur vents, lava flows, and cinder cones.

The wind and the digestive tracts of birds transported spores and seeds of plants to the Hawaiian Islands, which, because of their isolation, developed a unique flora and fauna. Some seventy species of native birds evolved from about fifteen species that made it to the islands from elsewhere. The Hawaiian goose, or nene, a ground-nesting bird that prefers to live on lightly vegetated lava flows, was brought to the point of extinction by rats and mongooses taken to the islands by humans. But it appears to be recovering.

The centerpiece of Haleakala National Park is Haleakala Crater, seven-and-a-half miles long, two-and-a-half miles wide, and one-half mile deep. Haleakala last erupted about 1790, not too long ago in volcanic terms, and it is probably not extinct, just dormant.

The most famous plant of the crater is the silversword, a two-foot-wide rosette with many dagger-like silvery leaves. Too attractive for its own good—humans pulled them up and goats ate them—the silverswords were near extinction at one time but they are now recovering under protection of the park. Once in its lifetime the silversword sends up a cluster of one hundred to five hundred yellow and purplish flowers on a stalk up to eight feet tall—and then the plant dies.

In contrast to the ash- and lava-covered surface of the crater, the Kipahulu section of the park offers rolling grasslands and forested valleys that drop sharply to the sea. The upper rain forest receives as much as 250 inches of rain a year. A chain of pools connected with waterfalls and cascades leads from the forest to the ocean.

On the U.S. mainland, the Cascade Mountains trace the path of the Ring of Fire through the Pacific Northwest. The southernmost volcano in the Cascades is Lassen Peak in northern California. Lassen Volcanic National Park was established in 1916 even as eruptions were continuing. The biggest explosion in a four-year sequence (1914-1917) occurred on May 22, 1915, when a release of lava and gas sent a mushroom cloud seven miles into the stratosphere.

Lassen, which had erupted many times, began as a vent on the flank of Mount Tehama, an immense volcano whose peak collapsed a long time ago into its own caldera. Though Lassen has remained quiet since a few final puffs in 1921, it is certainly not extinct. Meanwhile, scientists study the recovery of plant species in this outdoor laboratory. The young forest has proved in places to be even more diverse than the adult forest wiped out by the eruptions.

Tracing the Cascades to the north, the next park is in Oregon: Crater Lake, atop Mount Mazama, which William Steel had successfully promoted as a park.

In southern Washington state, Mount St. Helens was just one of many lovely snow-capped Cascade peaks until May 18, 1980, when a volcanic explosion of unimaginable force blew off the top thirteen hundred feet of the mountain and lofted a plume of smoke and ash fifteen miles into the sky.

Crater Lake National Park in Oregon was established to honor the deepest lake in the United States—1,932 feet. This lake began to form after a massive volcanic explosion blew off the top of Mount Mazama about seven thousand years ago. Wizard Island is a volcanic cone in its own right.

Mount Rainier, soaring in splendid isolation sixty miles southeast of Seattle, is a beloved symbol of Washington state. Tides of moist air flowing eastward from the Pacific bump into Rainier and deposit immense amounts of snow on its slopes.

Thousands of lava flows and volcanic eruptions have left Mount Rainier with a misshapen and somewhat battered appearance—no perfect cone, here. Rainier has been dormant since the mid-1800s, but geologists predict it will awaken sometime in the future.

A tide of glowing gas and rock and thick mud swept down the slopes, obliterating two hundred square miles of timber, lakes, and valley. Spirit Lake, a popular recreation area, became a desert. More than sixty persons died. Mount St. Helens National Volcanic Monument was established under the administration of the U.S. Forest Service.

The crowning glory of the Cascade Range is Mount Rainier, the beloved symbol of Washington state, rising 14,410 feet in isolated splendor, its snowfields visible from all directions for one hundred miles. Residents of Seattle and Tacoma may be forgiven for casting nervous glances at the volcano articulating their skyline. Rainier erupted in the 1800s and many times before that. Once, geologists believe, its peak was a perfect Mt. Fuji-style cone reaching to sixteen thousand feet in elevation, but ice sheets and an eruption some 5,800 years ago knocked off some of the summit and marred the symmetry. Twenty-seven glaciers have cut deeply into the slopes of Rainier, and they are separated by rock walls called cleavers.

Moist air flowing off the Pacific encounters nothing like this mountain. Clouds form and surrender about one hundred inches of precipitation a year, mostly in the form of snow. In winter, the three-story Paradise Inn, a popular spot for visitors in summer, may be buried up to its roof.

The peak of Mount Rainier is often obscured by clouds or fog, unless, of course, you are above the layers of white. The 14,410-foot mountain is a popular challenge for climbers, but more than fifty have died trying to reach the frozen summit.

In spring, meltwater pours off the mountain, in places carving enchanting, otherworldly ice caves.

At lower elevations, Douglas fir, red cedars, and western hemlock rise two hundred feet in a massive forest. Above the trees, the subalpine landscape offers colorful displays of raw beauty and open views of wildlife, including the delightful marmots, furry rodents who romp about, watch, whistle, and look over their two-footed visitors.

Volcanism played a role in the creation of the Olympic Range, now partly within Olympic National Park west of Seattle. The future home of the gods, Mount Olympus and its neighbors got their start 55 million years ago on the floor of the Pacific Ocean. Massive amounts of sediments were washed into the sea and compressed into shale and sandstone. Lava joined this mix, pouring forth from fissures in the earth's crust, and hardening into basalt. Underwater mountains—seamounts—formed. Later, the Pacific plate bearing these submerged mountains collided with the continental plate, another exciting physiographic event we missed by a mere thirty million years. A portion of the seamounts slid under the continental plate, but their tops piled up to become today's Olympic Range. Glaciers, the last of which retreated twelve thousand years ago, designed the present pattern of peaks and valleys. The glaciers carved Juan de Fuca Strait and Puget Sound, isolating the Olympics from the mainland.

The Olympics form a tight cluster, from which thirteen rivers tumble to the sea like spokes of a wheel. They are supplied by up to two hundred inches of annual precipitation. That's on the western side. The eastern side is nearly a desert.

A temperate rain forest, the nation's finest example, spreads westward at low elevations from the mountains to the Pacific Ocean. Sitka spruce is the principal tree of the forest. The dense canopy of trees catches snow that never reaches the ground. A carpet of moss absorbs sound, and the ambience in the subdued light is that of a cathedral. The composition of the forest changes with increases in elevation, and above the tree line the subalpine zone features flower-floored meadows.

Wildlife includes the shy Roosevelt elk, traveling in elusive herds, and mountain goats, an introduced species that seems to eat everything in sight. The Park Service is trying to figure out how to get rid of them.

The park encompasses fifty-seven miles of Pacific coastline. Sea stacks rise from the ocean, and the forest nearly meets the sea, enhancing the drama of this wild, isolated world of contact and conflict. Bears cruise the beach in search of food. Raccoons feed on shellfish at low tide. Birds are everywhere, inspecting what the sea has thrown them. Eagles circle overhead, oystercatchers pry open mussels with their long bills and turnstones turn stones in search of goodies underneath. Gulls drop clamshells from a height of fifty feet to crack them open on the rocks.

In the Hoh Rain Forest on Mount Olympus in Olympic National Park in Washington, the canopy is so thick that in some places falling snow is caught in the trees and never reaches the ground.

*Black-tailed mule deer,
Olympic National Park.
From the jumbled peaks,
thirteen rivers tumble
to the sea, and six hundred
miles of hiking trails provide
access to the lush forests.*

*Sea stacks are prominent on Ruby
Beach in Olympic National Park.
The Pacific surf tosses clams,
crabs, snails, mussels, and other
sea animals onto the beach, where
they are snapped up by shorebirds,
raccoons, bears, and bald eagles.*

Lava Beds National Monument contains nearly two hundred lava-tube caves that were formed after molten lava poured forth in volcanic eruptions. The outer surface of the lava cooled and hardened, and after the hot inner flow dissipated, the empty tubes remained.

Seattle invariably ranks near the top of lists naming the "best" places to live in the United States. Parklands nearly surround the city. The most rugged wilderness is found in the North Cascades National Park Service Complex northeast of Seattle. The complex includes the park as well as Ross Lake and Lake Chelan national recreation areas.

Complex is also a good word for the jumbled landforms of the North Cascades. A sort of geological tossed salad, the mountains offer up scenery for which no other experience has prepared the visitor. The writer and photographer Kim Heacox has observed, "Adjectives that worked elsewhere failed here, as if our language had evolved in a world without comparable scenery." Others have called the North Cascades "the American Alps."

To make a very long story short, sediments laid down half a billion years ago were rearranged by volcanism, erosion, and the movement of the earth's plates. Shallow seas deposited sediments, covering what was left. The cycle of mountain building and erosion repeated itself

several times. Magma burst out of the earth and spilled over the terrain, and two volcanic lava mountains, Baker and Glacier Peak (both outside the park) rose above the Cascade summits. The icefields moved in and out, leaving 318 glaciers in the park. The mountains are nearly impenetrable, and few people knew much about them before the park was established in 1968. The hardy few included members of mountain-climbing clubs.

The densely conifered western slope gets 110 inches of precipitation a year, yet a valley just to the east of the park gets only twelve inches. Major mammals, including mountain lions, bobcats, black bears, and mule deer, are well represented.

State Route 20 cuts through the complex to the reservoirs in the recreation areas and provides access to many trails leading into the wilderness. The glacier-carved and pencil-shaped Lake Chelan, fifty-five miles long and fifteen hundred feet deep, points into the wilderness. The trip up the lake and into the beyond is an exceptional experience.

Mount Shuskan, North Cascades National Park, in Washington. The park contains 318 glaciers, more than one-half of the total found in the forty-eight contiguous states. Access by car is limited, so the park belongs mostly to hikers and mountain climbers, for whom it is a mecca.

ALASKA

Early people called it Alyeshka—"The Great Land." Our northern subcontinent wins the gold in almost every competition in America's Landscape Olympics. Alaska has the biggest moose and bears, the tallest spruce, the tallest mountains, the largest glaciers, and simply more of almost every landform.

The land's youthful energy can be felt and measured, in mountains still pushing upward, in undammed rivers running free to the ocean, in the unrestrained movement of animal life—streambeds turn red with salmon, caribou flow across the tundra, mobs of mosquitoes persecute the caribou.

Glacier Bay National Park, in the panhandle of southeast Alaska, may be changing more rapidly than any of America's other crown jewels. Reminiscent of the dog that didn't bark, this is a story of the glacier that's not there.

The story begins with the start of the Little Ice Age about four thousand years ago. Glaciers formed as snowfall in the mountains exceeded snowmelt. Snowflakes changed to round ice grains and then, under mounting weight, to solid ice. Gravity moved the mass downslope, perhaps a few feet per day. Glaciers advanced in this area until about

A moose forages for food beneath the snow in Denali National Park. Unlike caribou, moose—which may weigh sixteen hundred pounds—do not travel in herds. They are stalked by secretive, seldom-seen packs of wolves.

McBride Glacier in Glacier Bay National Park, Alaska. McBride is among the glaciers that have been retreating in the park, apparently as a result of subtle changes in climate.

Riggs Glacier, in Glacier Bay National Park. In the park, tidewater glaciers reach down to the sea. Large slabs of ice frequently calve, or break off, from the glaciers and crash into the water.

1750, and then a meltdown began. The snout (front) of the bay's glacier began to retreat up the bay. When observed in 1794, Glacier Bay's snout still reached nearly to its mouth. No small affair, this glacier was four thousand feet thick and up to twenty miles wide, and it extended upbay more than one hundred miles to the mountains.

But in 1879 John Muir found that the ice had retreated forty-eight miles up the bay. Glacier Bay branches like a tree into a number of inlets, and most of their respective glaciers continue to fall back. No other glacier has been known to retreat so fast, and scientists are studying how this process may be related to subtle changes in climate.

The calving of glaciers is one of nature's showiest performances. Slabs of ice up to two hundred feet high break loose and crash into the water. An underwater slab may pop off, rush to the surface, and capsize unwary boaters.

From mountain tundra to the hemlock and spruce forest, the park provides sanctuary for a broad range of plants and animals. For most visitors, the biggest thrill is seeing a humpback whale, up to fifty feet long, surface briefly in the bay, then dive, its tail flukes standing tall for an instant before it disappears. Whales sing to each other, and maybe someday we will be able to decode their messages.

The St. Elias Mountains, in Wrangell-St. Elias National Park and Preserve. This park, at 13.2 million acres, is six times the size of Yellowstone and contains nine of the sixteen highest peaks in the United States.

A brown bear watches for salmon at Brooks Falls in Katmai National Park and Preserve. Each summer a million or more salmon return to Katmai's rivers and lakes from the Pacific Ocean. They swim toward the same gravel beds where they hatched two or three years before—and the bears and eagles are waiting.

Horned puffins occupy steep cliffs and rocky ledges along the coast of Kenai Fjords National Park. Kenai's bird populations were hard-hit by the oil spill in Prince William Sound in 1989.

Northwest of Glacier Bay, where Alaska's panhandle joins the pan, Wrangell-St. Elias National Park and Preserve soars out of the Gulf of Alaska. Six times the size of Yellowstone, Wrangell-St. Elias is by far the nation's largest park. Its other superlatives include the Bagley Ice Field, eighty miles long, and the nation's two biggest glaciers, one of them the size of Rhode Island—which it feeds. The St. Elias Mountains, with Mount Logan over the border in Canada reaching to 19,850 feet, are the world's tallest coastal mountains. Canyons rival Yosemite and Zion in size. The mineral wealth was bountiful. Silver was extensively mined in the future park, and the famed Kennecott mine, until it closed in 1938, yielded one billion pounds of copper.

The mighty Copper River forms the western boundary of Wrangell-St. Elias, and a major tributary, the glacier-fed Chitina River, is a superlative example of its kind. The Chitina flows from east to west, and its valley provides access by gravel road to the center of the park. Within its broad valley bottom, the Chitina spreads several miles wide, following a complex vine of channels and creating a classic Alaskan braided river.

Compact bands of the majestic all-white Dall sheep roam the high meadows and inhospitable ridgetops. As in other parks bearing the designation, the "preserve" sections are open to sport hunting of the sheep and other wildlife.

Rafting, hiking, cross-country skiing, and fishing opportunities are available, but much of this park is an unapproachable (for most of us) and icebound wilderness, and you might prefer just to stay home and watch the video.

Kenai Fjords National Park, on the Gulf of Alaska's west coast, is, in one way, a junior version of Wrangell. Its dominant feature is the Harding Ice Field, three hundred square miles spread across the Kenai Mountains. The mountains are nearly buried, their summits barely above the white sheets. The icefield is sustained by up to six hundred inches of annual snowfall.

Anyone planning a trek across the icefield should prepare for sudden storms, high winds, extreme temperature changes, and blinding sunlight bouncing off the snow. That's in the summer, when the going is easiest. In other seasons you might encounter real problems. Watch out for those nasty crevasses!

Tectonic plates collide along the coast, and, as one slides under the other, Kenai's coast is being dragged underwater, and the mountains now tilt into the sea. As alpine valleys fill with seawater, they become fjords, and these fingers of the gulf reach far inland. In a violent land, change can come quickly. In

The bald eagle, the American national bird, is the monarch of the skies over Denali National Park. The open terrain makes it easy for this sharp-eyed predator to spot small mammals down below.

1964, an earthquake twice as powerful as the 1906 San Francisco shocker devastated the nearby town of Seward and dropped the Kenai shoreline six feet in one day.

Bears prowl the narrow inhabitable strip of coast, and sea life in quantity occupies the shore and the nearby islands. Sea otters, once hunted nearly to extinction, cavort in protected safety. About 175,000 seabirds have staked out their turf and cling to their few rocky inches of the American Dream. Gulls, puffins, and kittiwakes put on quite a show, and bald eagles nest in the tops of spruce and hemlock trees. Prince William Sound lies to the northeast, and the calamitous oil spill there in 1989 spread south toward the Kenai coast, with devastating consequences for its wildlife.

The peaks of the Aleutian Range are anchored to the mainland to the east, and to the west they dip into the sea as the Aleutian Islands. These are restless, living mountains, very much a part of the Ring of Fire. Near the head of the Aleutian Peninsula, a week of earthquakes in early June, 1912, had signaled disquiet down below, and the few people living in the immediate area cleared out.

But the sunny morning of June 6 gave no promise that darkness would fall at the noon hour, that the most violent day on earth in the last 3,500 years of recorded history was at hand. At 1 PM, with a thunderclap of sound heard seven hundred miles away, a small vent at the foot of Mount Katmai

began to eject seven cubic miles of volcanic vomit, a flood of incandescent sand and gas that inundated, to a depth of seven hundred feet, a valley fifteen miles long and three to six miles wide.

A black tide of airborne ash rolled southeast. At a fishing camp thirty miles distant, a man wrote his wife, "We are awaiting death at any minute. ... Here are darkness and hell, thunder and noise. I do not know whether it is day or night." In Kodiak, one hundred miles from Mount Katmai, a lantern held at arm's length could not be seen for two days. The eruption, ten times more powerful than the one at Mount St. Helens, hazed most of the Northern Hemisphere, and the reduced sunshine cooled the summer.

Members of a National Geographic Society expedition found a crater lake on Mount Katmai and thought that the summit was the source of the eruption. Not so, however. Most of the release came from Novarupta, a mere pimple at the edge of the valley, just two hundred feet high. Magma ejected from Novarupta was drained from under Mount Katmai, whose summit then subsided, leaving the caldera in which the lake formed.

The volcanic ash and sand that spread across the valley interacted with buried rivers to produce one of nature's most sinister spectacles. Everywhere one looked, steam rose from vents in the ground in

Dall sheep are common in Denali. In spring they graze at lower elevations and follow the snowmelt up the mountains as summer progresses.

The three-hundred-square-mile Harding Ice Field in Kenai Fjords National Park has virtually no features aside from the occasional nunatak (Eskimo for "lone peak") that projects above the ice.

The peaks of Denali, a lure to experienced climbers, present one of the ultimate tests of human courage and endurance. Storms, which can occur without warning, have trapped climbers, sometimes fatally.

this newly named "Valley of Ten Thousand Smokes." The smoke fizzled out within thirty years, and the volcanic deposits consolidated into *tuff*, a form of soft, porous rock. Creeks have cut deep canyons within the tuff. But Novarupta still exhales steam from its mouth, its breathing as ominous as that of a horror film slasher.

Today this great park, accessible only by plane and boat, is an untouched wilderness, ruled by the nation's largest grizzlies. At up to fifteen hundred pounds in weight, they are the world's largest predators on land. They reach great size because they dine on migrating salmon. In one of nature's most dramatic demonstrations of the power of instinct, salmon return from the sea by the millions, stop eating, turn red in color, and swim up rivers to the graveled streambeds of their birth, to spawn and die and provide food for bears and eagles.

The wildlife in the park's lakes and forests and along its many bayfronts is bountiful. Katmai has room for one to roam, to inhale the freshness of unsullied nature and to experience what writer Susan Tollefson has called "that indescribable feeling one has when traveling alone and unarmed through raw, rugged, unpeopled country."

The Ring of Fire continues to the northeast of Katmai, and some of its major ramparts are included in Lake Clark National Park and Preserve. The mountains in the park are the Chigmits, products of various geological processes. Two active volcanoes, Iliamna and Redoubt, let off steam from time to time.

Caribou eat their way through the valley below the Alaska Range. Denali is a wildlife park, and animals are easy to spot in the broad open terrain. Thirty-seven species of mammals are found in the park.

The park was established in part to protect the sockeye salmon, which make their annual "run" here in prodigious numbers, some 35 million in 1981, for example. Showing an amazing ability to meet deadlines—and this is their ultimate deadline—the sockeye assemble off the coast in early summer, having swum there from thousands of miles away. They proceed to Iliamna Lake and then to the particular streambed where they were spawned.

This roadless wilderness of tundra, lake, and forest actually has a short trail, which leads from Lake Clark, near the airstrip, to Tanalian Falls, four miles round-trip. Other than that, you're on your own, through fields of boulders, bogs, quicksand, and slippery slopes. This excursion is not for the inexperienced, or for anyone incapable of experiencing a transcendent moment. Three of the nation's officially designated wild rivers are within the park, and they lead floating transients past moose and beaver dams, waterfalls and waterfowl sanctuaries, and down challenging rapids.

Still farther north, the Aleutian Range terminates, jammed up against the Alaska Range, the six hundred-mile arc of mountains that separates south central Alaska from the interior plateau to the north. The Alaska Range formed along the path of the Denali Fault, where the earth buckled, fractured, and folded. Blocks of the crust lifted up to form mountains, and underneath a chamber of magma cooled gradually into granite. The granite, too, was pushed up, breaching the surface and forming an awesome massif that ultimately surpassed the older mountains.

The colossus that rises in lofty isolation from its neighbors, more than three miles above its base, was called Denali, "the High One," by the Athabascans. The name is perpetuated in "Denali National Park and Preserve," but the mountain itself bears the name given it in 1896 by a prospector, as a tribute to a senator who had just been nominated for president, William McKinley.

Ice, hundreds of feet thick in places, overlies the granite core of Mount McKinley. Permanent snowfields cover more than half of the mountain, and glaciers carve its flanks. A temperature of -95°F has been recorded on the mountain, and winds can gust to 150 miles an hour. More often than not in summer, the High One is concealed behind a cloud cover.

The many glaciers that flow off Mount McKinley and its neighbors feed magnificent examples of braided rivers, which spread out across valleys, unable

Each summer in Denali a thin layer of topsoil thaws out and is able to support life. The tundra, shown here in the fall, is home to dwarfed shrubs and miniaturized wildflowers that have adapted to a short growing season.

Transporting cold water from the glaciers of the Alaska Range, the Toklat River flows across Denali. Because the permafrost, just beneath the surface of the ground, is so hard, rivers cannot cut deep channels, and instead they split into a number of shallow "braids"; thus they are referred to as "braided rivers."

to form deep channels because of the underlying permafrost.

In the lowlands, the principal ecological divisions are *taiga* and tundra. Taiga, a Russian word, means "land of little sticks." The sticks, which flourish mostly in the river valleys, are stunted versions of aspen, birch, poplar, and spruce. Above the valleys, the tundra begins at elevations of two thousand feet. Here, dwarfed shrubs and miniaturized flowers adjust to the short growing season. Despite their small size, they are vitally important as a source of nutrients for the wildlife.

Because of the vast open terrain (in a park larger than Massachusetts), wildlife can be seen easily. Herds of caribou often approach the park road, while the solitary moose feeds on willows along streams. Wolves are about, but more wary. Dall sheep, their white coats and yellow horns making them one of nature's handsomest animals, negotiate the high rocky slopes. Omnivorous grizzly bears, consuming plants, berries, squirrels, moose, caribou calves, and carrion with equal gusto, ramble through the park.

A few bird species, including raven, ptarmigan, magpie, and gray jay, winter here, but most birds stay only for the summer. In what has to be the world's longest commute, the Arctic tern flies in each year from Antarctica.

Four park areas lie north of the Arctic Circle. In the west, bordering Kotzebue Sound, Cape Krusenstern National Monument protects the sites of artifacts that trace the history of human hunting of

Lake Clark National Park and Preserve is a roadless region where backpackers can roam virtually at will for weeks through flowered alpine tundra and rolling hills, past pristine lakes and smoking volcanoes.

marine mammals over a span of six thousand years. Noatak National Preserve contains the nation's largest untouched river basin. Flowing from glacial melt on Mount Igikpak in the Brooks Range, the Noatak River has cut the scenic Grand Canyon of the Noatak, a migration route for animals and canoeists and kayakers who float placidly in summer and camp at "night" under the midnight sun.

Waterborne travel on the Kobuk and Salmon rivers is *de rigueur* in Kobuk Valley National Park, which is served by no dirt roads, much less an interstate highway. Mountains bracket the valley, but the river brings explorers close to the park's most unusual feature—the Great Kobuk Sand Dunes, twenty-five square miles of rounded, frosted grains of quartzite and other minerals. The dune field, the largest above the Arctic Circle, seems Arizonan in summer when temperatures can hit 100°F. Dunes rise to one hundred feet.

The tide of barren-ground caribou crosses the Kobuk River twice yearly, and for an astonishing 12,500 years—according to archaeological evidence—humans have been waiting at a place called Onion Portage to kill a few of the animals for food and clothing. This use of the caribou by Natives on a subsistence basis is still allowed.

The Brooks Range, running west from Canada, is the northernmost extension of the Rocky Mountains, and a portion of the central Brooks Range lies within Gates of the Arctic National Park

The row of peaks in the Alaska Range, in the middle distance, is overwhelmed by Mount McKinley, which soars into the alpenglow and clouds to an altitude of 20,320 feet. McKinley, in Denali National Park and Preserve, is the highest mountain in the United States.

and Preserve. The National Park Service calls Gates of the Arctic "America's ultimate wilderness." Encompassing 8,400,000 acres, much of it in gentle valleys, Gates has more explorable land than any other park. The exploration does not come without planning, however. Aside from an absence of roads, there aren't even any trails in a park two hundred miles wide, and access is by charter plane.

Such prominent spires as Mount Igikpak and the Arrigetch Peaks are formed in granite, the product of volcanic action, but many other summits are in limestone. The comings and goings of the glacial sheets have left a sculptured wonderland of U-shaped valleys, hanging valleys, tarns, and cirques. Moraines have helped form mountain lakes. Runoff from rain spills swiftly over the permanently frozen ground.

Robert Marshall, a founder of the Wilderness Society who explored the Brooks Range in the 1930s and wrote lyrically in its behalf, came up with the idea for the park's name. He saw two massive peaks, Frigid Crags and Boreal Mountain, stationed on either side of the North Fork of the Koyukuk River, as the gates to the northland.

Taiga gives way on the north slope of the Brooks Range to tundra that stretches up to the Arctic Ocean, a carpet of heath, grass, sedge, moss, and lichen in never-ending patterns of growth.

Gates of the Arctic National Park and Preserve is north of the Arctic Circle. In a vast inland empire of mountain and valley, of river and tundra, lovers of nature who have explored all other landscapes and met all other challenges outdoors can visit this wilderness at the edge of the world and rejoice at the freedom it confers upon us.

The flowering season is brief but intense. Although the caribou herds pass this way, too, animal life is otherwise widely distributed because of the scarcity of edible plants. But 130 kinds of birds have been seen, and trout, grayling, and pike are found in the lakes and streams.

After fingering those glossy brochures describing the delights of Acapulco, consider a park that has something for everyone: perpetual daylight, perpetual darkness, temperatures ranging from 90°F to -70°F, wolves, bears, rainbows, the aurora borealis, and an absolute freedom most people have never known. In truth the park is for everyone, and not just for those few who commit themselves to it physically. New Yorkers who don't even get to the Statue of Liberty want to know that it is there, and we all need to know that a place like Gates of the Arctic is there, an escape of last resort from whatever stress civilization has imposed upon us, a gift to ourselves to cherish and treasure forever.

The aurora borealis in the sky above Denali. The aurora occurs when charged particles from the sun strike the upper atmosphere near the magnetic poles.

PHOTO CREDITS